OUR STORY

The Rossport 5

OUR STORY

The Rossport 5

small world media

SMALL WORLD MEDIA
Knocknaquirk
Magheramore
County Wicklow

Trade enquiries to
087 955 1504 (Ireland)
07816 146 567 (Britain)

ISBN 13: 978 0 9554634 0 2
ISBN: 0 9554634 0 8

A CIP record for this book is
available from the British Library

Cover and book design: Seanchai MultiMedia
Photography: John Monaghan

Printed by La Fotocomposizione, Torino

CONTENTS

CHRONOLOGY

1996
OCTOBER Corrib field is discovered by Enterprise Oil 70 kilometres off Mayo coast.

2000
OCTOBER Bord Gáis outlines plans to construct a pipeline from north Mayo to Craughwell, County Galway, on behalf of the Corrib co-venturers – Enterprise Oil, Statoil and Marathon.

NOVEMBER Enterprise Energy Ireland (EEI) applies for planning permission for an onshore gas processing plant at Ballanaboy, north Mayo.

2001
JANUARY Mayo County Council seeks more information from EEI.

APRIL EEI submits a new planning application.

AUGUST 3 At five o'clock on the Bank Holiday Friday Mayo County Council announces that it has granted planning permission for the onshore processing plant. This is immediately appealed to An Bord Pleanála by residents and environmental groups.

AUGUST 24 Minister for the Marine Frank Fahey, during a debate on Corrib gas, tells the Humbert Summer School in Ballina that the objectors are holding up progress in the west.

OCTOBER The Minister for the Marine denies claims made in the Dáil by Mayo Fine Gael TD, Michael Ring, that he has been interfering in the planning process in relation to the Corrib project.

NOVEMBER 16 Minister Fahey issues a petroleum lease for the gas field.

NOVEMBER 21 EEI applies for approval of its Plan of Development, a Foreshore Licence, and consent to construct the production pipeline.

2002
FEBRUARY An Bord Pleanála opens its oral hearing in Ballina on the appeal against planning permission for the onshore processing plant.

APRIL Minister Fahey publishes the Marine Licence Vetting Committee report, which recommends granting full consents to the Corrib project. It does not address a shallow-water, offshore processing option for the gas.

The Plan of Development for the Corrib gas project is approved.

MAY Foreshore licence granted by Minister Fahey to EEI shortly before he leaves office.

JUNE An Bord Pleanála requests further information on the onshore processing plant application from EEI, now owned by Shell, and raises concerns about health and safety. It asks the company to consider shallow-water   processing of the gas.

NOVEMBER An Bord Pleanála holds an unprecedented second oral hearing into the Shell application. The two oral hearings have now lasted 22 days, making them the second longest in the board's history.

DECEMBER Shell and now former Minister Fahey deny claims in a Channel 4 news report that 'huge pressure' was exerted on Mayo County Council's planning office to grant permission for the controversial onshore processing plant.

2003
APRIL An Bord Pleanála's Inspector concludes that the processing plant is the wrong project in the wrong place. He delivers a comprehensive, damning report on the project. The Board overturns Mayo County Council's decision to grant planning permission for the gas processing plant on the narrower grounds of the peat deposition methods being used by Shell. Political pressure, led by Frank Fahey and Enda Kenny, is immediately applied to ensure a new application is made.

SEPTEMBER Senior executives from the consortium meet with the Taoiseach and a number of ministers to get assurances on the government's support for the Corrib project. On the same day over twenty serious bogslides occur on Dooncarton mountain, which overlooks the route of Shell's proposed production pipeline. Days later the oil and gas lobby group in Ireland, which includes Shell, make a presentation on the importance of the Corrib gas project to An Bord Pleanála.

DECEMBER A new planning application is submitted by Shell. It includes revised plans for the removal of large quantities of peat from the gas processing site.

2004
APRIL Mayo County Council grants planning permission subject to a total of 75 conditions. Local people immediately indicate that they intend to appeal the decision to An Bord Pleanála.

OCTOBER Shell is granted planning permission by An Bord Pleanála for the Ballanaboy gas processing plant. On this occasion, no oral hearing was held.

2005

APRIL Proceedings are instituted in the High Court to prevent residents obstructing the construction of the gas pipeline at Rossport. The High Court grants Shell the right to access private lands in the village for the installation of the pipeline.

JUNE Five residents from Rossport are jailed for contempt of court for refusing to obey the High Court order not to interfere with the construction of the Corrib gas pipeline. The men vow to stay in prison until they get justice. An immediate campaign begins causing the suspension of all Shell work activity in north Mayo. Large rallies in support of the men are held throughout the country.

SEPTEMBER After 94 days in Cloverhill prison, Shell drops the injunction and the five men are released. They and their supporters vow that their campaign will go on. After a number of controversial 'independent' safety reviews, most notably one by a company jointly owned by Shell, the Government appoints the British firm Advantica to review the safety of Shell's production pipeline.

NOVEMBER The government appoints Peter Cassells to act as mediator between the five men and Shell to help resolve all differences between the sides.

2006

MARCH The Advantica report is published and recommends that the production pipeline pressure be capped at 144 bar if technically possible. The report is unable under its Terms of Reference to address alternative routes or alternative ways of processing the gas.

JULY Peter Cassells brings mediation to an end declaring that the two sides are too far apart and agreement is unlikely. He issues a report suggesting adjustments to the route of the production pipeline. He is unable under his Terms of Reference to address the question of the onshore gas processing plant or recommend alternative processing methods.

OCTOBER Shell forcibly resumes work on constructing the processing plant. A large force of Gardai is deployed. There are daily protests by local people.

Introduction

Mark Garavan

On September 30, 2005 five men were discharged from prison by the High Court in Dublin. They had served 94 days in Cloverhill prison for refusing to obey a court order directing them not to interfere with work on the proposed Shell pipeline in north Mayo.

When they entered prison on June 29 they were almost entirely unknown outside a cluster of small villages and communities. By the time they left prison they had become figures of national and, even to some extent, international prominence. Five quiet and private individuals had become the 'Rossport Five'. They were men who had brought the 900 million euro Shell project in Mayo to a complete halt.

The courtroom from which they were discharged was packed with their families, supporters, media and politicians. There was barely standing room. When the men emerged into the hall of the Four Courts they were enveloped in an excited crowd of well-wishers. Outside the court, dozens of journalists and cameramen fought to record their initial comments. Large crowds were gathered. The men were accompanied in their walk to the cameras by nearly twenty TDs.

The men had entered a different world from that of 94 days previously. Then, the scenes both inside and outside the court were nothing short of horrific. People lay on the footpath overcome with grief and despair. Others stood shocked and numbed that peaceful protest could have resulted in an indefinite prison sentence. When the men entered prison, the Corrib gas project seemed a done deal, certain to go ahead. No one was paying any attention to the demands of locals. Shell had already begun work on excavating peat from the site of their proposed gas processing plant.

However, by the time the men were released all of this had changed. The following day the men led a crowd of 5,000 people through the streets of Dublin. That evening, in the early hours of the morning, they returned to Mayo greeted by bonfires and many hundreds of their neighbours.

The battle against the Corrib gas project had begun in the autumn of 2000. There were many acts and dramas in the long campaign to get the project re-configured to accommodate local concerns and fears. The release of the men from prison was merely the end of one further scene in this protracted and extraordinary battle between residents in a number of small villages and some of the most powerful oil and gas corporations in the world fully supported by the Irish government.

The focus on the men may have obscured the extraordinary events which had unfolded in north Mayo through the summer of 2005. In effect, a local community had revolted and refused to accept a development project that they felt had been imposed on the area. Their refusal was such that irrespective of the law, irrespective of the consequences to themselves, they brought the entire Shell project to a stop.

There are thus many books that could be written about the Corrib gas conflict. There is the story of the community revolt, the story of the men's families, particularly their wives, who found themselves carrying much of the burden of the public campaign in their absence, and the story of the other local landowners who had refused consent to Shell such as Monica Muller and Bríd McGarry.

This book simply sets out to tell part of the story through the voices of the five men who were imprisoned. It does not purport to offer a comprehensive account of all events nor does it seek to detail the technical objections and analyses that animated the men's opposition. Those matters are for another occasion and a different format. Instead, the attention in this book is on the men's direct experiences at the hands of Shell and the Irish State.

What emerges is a tale of resistance to power, of resistance to being treated as objects without a voice. It is tale of a refusal to being exposed to unacceptable levels of risk, a refusal to allow families, community and place be diminished and threatened for the profits of a multi-national corporation. But it is also a tale of the affirmation of community values, of safety, of democracy.

Much more was at stake in this conflict than might have been apparent to the casual observer. At issue was the quality of Irish democracy, the integrity of Irish administration, the power and responsibilities of global corporations, environmental well-being and the rights of citizens to dissent and protect themselves from threat. The Corrib gas campaign has brought into vivid relief issues and concerns felt by many in contemporary Ireland and throughout the world. North Mayo has the potential to become Ireland's Chiapas.

At the heart of the men's opposition was their profound sense that the insertion of a huge processing plant and associated pipelines into their community, without any participation from themselves and without any long-term benefit, would irrevocably transform their place from a locale of intimacy and familiarity to something threatening and alien. Therefore, to understand the Corrib gas conflict you have to see the world in a particular way. You have to know the value of place and what that means. You have to know what it is to feel invaded, to be afraid and to have no power to resist. You have to know what it is like to be ignored, to be ridiculed.

In north Mayo people fought back and refused to allow their place be taken from them. This therefore is a story of optimism in a world of growing ecological decline and political disengagement.

Yet neither the community nor the five men who went to prison were heroes. These were ordinary people caught in an extraordinary situation. They did not seek out this position – these events were thrust upon them. Everything that they did they did because they felt they had no choice. They opposed the Shell project because they believed that they had to do so in order to protect themselves and their families. The five men resisted Shell's efforts to access lands in the village of Rossport because this was the logical consequence of their opposition to the project. They broke an order of the court because that was the logical inevitability of continuing to protect themselves. They accepted imprisonment because they believed that they could not agree to cease their opposition. They remained in prison indefinitely because they could not accept that they must accede to Shell's project. People in their villages brought Shell's work to an end, risking imprisonment themselves, because they could not permit their neighbours to be incarcerated while Shell's project was permitted to proceed. Thus everything was driven by necessity and events. If this was heroism it was heroism of the ordinary kind, heroism that all people are capable of when they feel left without choice.

In maintaining their opposition to the project in the face of the possibility that their homes and farms might be seized or that they would be imprisoned indefinitely the men stood by their opposition and were prepared to accept any sanction. This standard of commitment had a galvanising effect on the wider local community and demonstrated that opposition to the Shell project was grounded on conviction and principle. This forced a re-evaluation of the merits of the project on the part of many who previously might have been indifferent.

The public ethos of the men, their families and supporters which conveyed integrity and justice drew a compassionate response within the local community and wider afield. The sincerity and patent genuineness of the men's wives (whether one agreed with their position or not) struck a chord. The horrific scenes at the High Court following the men's imprisonment where terrible manifestations of grief and distress were recorded by journalists and photographers produced searing images which created an indelible impression. Bonds of communal solidarity were reinforced in the face of this action by an outside agent.

The temptation is to make more of these events than they deserve. But so too is the temptation to make less. The events may have been triggered ostensibly by a single issue but showing through is the enduring quality of the human spirit. We live in a cynical age where motives are constantly questioned and where value is nearly always measured in monetary terms. From the beginning of the Corrib gas conflict, the concerns of locals were dismissed by crude stereotypes. They were accused of seeking greater financial compensation. They were accused of not understanding what Shell was proposing. They were accused of being left-wing ideologues. They were accused of being luddites and anti-progress. The Corrib gas project itself was imbued with some of the most dominant myths of modernity, that industrialisation equals development, that industrial development equals progress, that fossil fuels must always be exploited.

In resisting these stereotypes and myths one can discern in this campaign a progression from an initial reaction to the gas proposal towards an affirmation of a particular set of values. It is in this sense that the north Mayo protests were not simply defensive and reactive. They were also assertions of autonomy, participation, and democratic rights. In short, people insisted that they had a legitimate view of their own and a distinct version of what constitutes development and modernisation.

I believe that the authentic voice of the Rossport Five heard in this book will stir the conscience of all who read it. Their story is presented so that others may have hope that they too can shape the world in which they live.

Finally, a word on method. Interviews for this book were conducted with four of the men and their wives in single sittings between June and August 2006. The interviews were recorded and transcribed by me. The transcripts were returned to the men and edited by them. Brendan Philbin wrote his chapter as a direct text.

Mark Garavan
September 2006

CHAPTER 1

'It would be the end of our life if Shell got in here'

Willie and Mary Corduff

BACKGROUND

WILLIE I was born and reared on this farm. It's memories that are making us do what we are doing. My father came here in 1947. The place then was pure bog with a fallen-down house. The memories we have are of the way we were brought up. Hard times. They're the memories you have and the memories you have to keep.

To see someone coming in now and trying to destroy it, as Shell is doing, it kills you. Our footsteps are around the place since we were able to walk. There are memories of our fathers and mothers and how hard they worked to bring us up. This was all bog land. It all had to be reclaimed by hand. Doing corners by spade and shaking a bit of their own seed that the cows had left after them in the shed. It wasn't that they went out and bought seed for they couldn't afford to go out and buy seed. They gathered up the seed that was left after the cow had eaten. They shook it in a corner every year to make it green. That's the reality. It's all memories. You cannot let them die.

I've only been out of this place for about a month. I went to Dublin. I had left school young and worked cutting seaweed and cutting turf, trying to live. You gave whatever money you had to your parents when you got it. I thought I could go away to Dublin and work on the buildings. I thought I could get a bit more money and get it easier. What we were at here at that stage there was no money in it, you just existed. My mother kept writing to me. I got a letter twice a week saying come home, please. They were heartbroken. So I felt I'd go home and that was it. I never left. I was glad to be back. Much as she wanted me back I was glad to be back. Because I didn't like it there. I worked on the buildings which I liked. I liked outside work. I was used to hard work. At the same time it was different work from what I was used to.

There were five in my family, three girls and two boys. I was the oldest boy. The girls were older. The girls were gone away at this stage. My younger brother was here at the time. My sisters had left home.

The work here you just slaved into it and hoped that it worked out all right. Hoped the weather was going to be good to dry the turf for sale. It was on turf that we survived. We grew our own potatoes and oats. Everything we had was our own. Because you couldn't afford to buy anything at the time. Everybody had their own at that time. You kept hens, you kept pigs, you had to be self-sufficient to live.

There wasn't much travelling about. I mean at most people would go to Belmullet on a fair day by bicycle to get a few things, like at springtime to get plants and that kind of thing for setting. But that was it. They'd go across the strand. That's the way they used to go to town to make it early and shorten the journey. They'd be gone to town that day and that was it. It'd be a month again before they'd go. They'd go every month if they could. But that was the only outing you got.

People's circumstances in Erris were all the same. My father and everybody else's father were the same. There was no such thing as somebody having more than the other. They shared everything they had. They got eggs from each other for putting down clutches, that type of thing. That was the reality. They used to swap, change potatoes for seed potatoes, so as to change the seed from different lands because you'd get a better crop. It wasn't that they used to buy them. They couldn't afford to buy a change of seed. You'd go for a few miles to get different seeds. It was a whole way of life.

We didn't know about Castlebar and Ballina. You'd hear of

somebody going to Ballina maybe once a year. The most would be twice a year. I don't think I ever remembered Castlebar when I was young. Castlebar in our time was nearly the same as America now. People used have to go to Castlebar for the hospital. If you heard that time of somebody going to Castlebar it was for being sick.

MARY As hard and all as the life sounds, there was one thing that came out above all – they were very happy. They were very contented people. They survived off the land and the sea and they didn't need to go elsewhere. The community spirit was there and they lived with each other and for each other. That's something that is changing today. That's the kind of thing people grew up with, that spirit. They were very happy even though they had nothing as in material things but they were very happy people. I remember Willie's father and mother here, a happier couple you didn't know.

WILLIE Mary is from across the bay about twelve miles away and from the same village as my mother. My father was born in Rossport and came from the other end of the village. He got married in 1946. He went to England and my mother stayed at home so he wanted to come back over. He had to borrow the money from his brother Druie to buy this place.

They didn't take life as being hard. They were very happy. That was the way of life. They took their clothes to a well on the shore to wash them. There was no water, there were no toilets. Those are the kind of times we grew up with and we're not that old! I mean you had nothing as such. But we were happy. Now, they have loads of things, yet they're not happy. If we got a spin on our father or mother's bicycle that time it was like now getting a spin in a helicopter. That's what it was like to us. Because you would not be let near their bicycle. They kept that safe. You'd have to ask for it if you wanted it for a spin. It was their only means of transport if, say, they had to go for a doctor. Kids that time were born in the house. You'd be looking forward to those kinds of things. There'd be a small bit of a party, you got extra things. The neighbours would be in.

My father and I worked here together all of the time. We built sheds which improved things. We borrowed money trying to improve ourselves. But after Mary and I were married a few years we had a huge fire which took everything we had which was very disheartening. The kids were young. We had a big choice then whether to stick at it. That was a big choice. And we did think about it. We were here left with six young kids. No income as such. So I mean where do we go now? Money borrowed. What we had borrowed long gone. So at night we'd talk about what were we going to do. But I just couldn't leave. It was hardship again for us trying to scrape up a few bob here and there. There was no work as such that you could go to. Where would you go, you'd have to go too far in that time to get work. I was working with the council when I left school, myself and a neighbour, on the roads. We had to cycle. We worked on the Glenamoy road, we used to cycle there. We were offered work elsewhere with them but we needed a car to get there. But we couldn't afford a car. So we had to stay at home and go on the dole. That's what we had to do. That's the way we survived. So if we could have afforded to get a car at that stage we'd probably still be working but we couldn't. That's what left us at home you could say.

We stuck it out after the fire but it was very, very hard. You just imagine bringing up six kids waiting on your dole and social welfare to come. It was very hard. There were horrible sacrifices we had to make. We cut turf. We had to. We used to cut seaweed, just to survive, to barely survive. The only way we did survive was we had our own potatoes and our own milk, which helped us along. I went fishing for three years then and I'd say they were the worst three years that ever came in the fishing! The catches were bad.

That fire was nearly the finish of me but I always said we were young and healthy to go on here and thankfully we did. Our neighbours and friends were very good to us and helped out in any way they could. Again, that community spirit was there and I believe it always will, a part of country life that Shell don't understand.

MARY But all that torture makes you a stronger person. It makes you value the real things of life. The more those kind of things happen it does make you a better kind of person.

WILLIE I just cannot walk away from here and leave it to Shell. I might as well die here with Shell as to go. Because I would die anyway if I had to leave with the memories I have of here.

WHAT WAS THE FIRST WORD ON THE GAS
PROJECT, THE FIRST INKLING LOCALLY?

WILLIE At first we were naïve. You wouldn't take a lot of notice of those things. We heard that there was gas found and it was coming in to Erris or Mayo somewhere. Later, we heard it was coming in to Aghoose, over on the Pollathomas side of the estuary. Enterprise Energy were doing surveys there. Then a fellow came from that company in the summer of 2000 and docked on our own doorstep and started telling us.

MARY It started to be announced in our Parish Newsletter that gas is coming to Erris and that anyone with ideas or questions could contact the parish priest.

There was also a petition or survey with The Western People which an awful lot of people signed saying how good this was. It was almost like the signatures that were given for the access to the pipeline – a lot of people signed it that didn't ask any questions about it.

WILLIE The news was coming first from the Church. Enterprise had their work done for years before they did announce anything. They did their homework the right way at the beginning.

MARY The company used the parish priest and the bishop. I remember the bishop saying on local radio that the gas coming in here was a godsend. People in Nigeria would never class an oil and gas company coming into an area as a godsend!

WILLIE They knew the people better than the people knew themselves. That's the way I look at it. They went to the right people. For rural Ireland the Church was always right. You could not change the people on that. They went to Mass every time there was Mass.

They went to nine Fridays. No matter how busy they were or what they were at. They had to either walk or cycle. It could be shining down sun and the hay in the field and if tomorrow it would be raining they'd still go to the church. So it was the news about the gas coming from the Church that convinced a lot of people.

MARY Enterprise had a 'presentation day' in a local pub, on the other side of the estuary in Pollathomas. That's where the pipe was supposed to be coming in at the beginning. That's what I call it – a 'presentation day' not a 'consultation day'. That's all that we heard about it, along with the Church bulletins. So they seemed to be in contact with the Church at all times.

WILLIE The parish priest in particular was the first to be talking about it. He announced it from the altar. He gave the impression to the people that your poverty is over. Even the company brought him and our bishop at the time out on a trip by helicopter to the gas field. The story was captured on TV and the newspapers.

MARY Maybe he thought it himself. I think maybe they were used.

WILLIE They were used big time and they were told that whatever was going to be needed in the area this was going to be the answer to it. I'd say that's what really happened. The people heard the parish priest announcing this from the altar, that poverty was over. You just take it that if you were in poverty for thirty or forty years, struggling to live, with hard work, and you have nothing, and to hear the parish priest coming to the altar saying this is it, it's over. The benefits that were going to be from it were going to be unreal.

MARY He then proposed that there be meetings on the gas involving all the groups in the area. You couldn't participate in this thing to do with the oil company unless you belonged to a group! I don't know if that was his idea or the company's.

WILLIE They set up The One Voice for Erris group. Funny enough, we went to it. Why, I don't know.

MARY We went because we had some doubt about the whole thing. I don't know what it was with hindsight but something always guided us. I don't know what it was.

WILLIE I don't know what it was. The only thing I always thought of was – why is it coming to us? Why is Erris getting it?

Because Erris never got anything easy that benefited it. Anything Erris ever got it had to be begged for or it had to be rallied for. So when you'd think of it you'd say why are we getting this now so easy without any aggro or without anyone looking for it. We thought at the time that nobody did look for it but with hindsight now looking back it was looked for. Hearing now what's going on I think some of the clergy had looked for it.

MARY They used the Church and the politicians to bring it in here. You blame so much of it on the politicians as well because they had this cry – they still have – 'we have nothing here'. They were saying this at all times – we have nothing. If you were an oil company out there well this was a perfect opportunity. Here they are – any crumb will do them. I blame politicians for this awful scourge being brought on the people here. They fed out the line all the time – 'we have nothing'. You'd nearly think they did it deliberately. If they had only put their heads together and worked on the things we do have here naturally and had forgotten about trying to destroy the area. We have fantastic opportunities here. We can create the right opportunities. If I was an oil company out there I'd say well this is a great opportunity to use the people, use the area, use their land, their water. That's one other reason why it was brought in this direction.

WILLIE We went along to the One Voice meeting to find out what was happening. What made us go to the meeting was that the pipe was now going through Rossport. We thought that now it is going to affect us.

WHAT WERE YOUR FIRST CONTACTS WITH THE ENTERPRISE?

MARY They first called to us at the beginning of August 2000. You felt that they had sent out letters about it. You got such an impression from the guy who called that you thought, hold on a minute, I didn't get any letter last week or did I miss something? Then you thought that all the others must have got their letters but they must have missed out on my mail. Then again, when you asked this neighbour and that neighbour and you talked to them, nobody got any word about it happening here. So they kind of used one neighbour off against the next. Coming here to my door saying well we've been at your neighbours, and coming to them and saying they were at us.

This is what they did. They were schooled in this. Their people were trained in how to react to people and how to work on people's minds that this is what they did. The psychology training that the company had was unreal. One example was when they first came to the area they would wave or salute you. Now, in our area people driving along the road always salute each other. It was a custom around here.

Now we were seeing complete strangers from other countries salute us as though they lived here all their lives. Of course they tried to become native! This is the same company who asked the courts to jail the men.

Later, they had one 'presentation' meeting out in a local pub at our request. That was how we got to know about them coming this side of the estuary with the pipe.

WILLIE I wasn't here when he called at first. I'd gone for the kids so Mary told him I'd be back at three o'clock. So he left and came back again in good time.

He was out there and shook hands with me. He was a Scottish man. He admired the cats and the dogs and the hens and chickens and whatever was around the place. Then he said, 'you know why I'm here'. I said, 'not really'. 'Ah well, you've probably heard about the gas'. 'Yeah', I said, 'but I didn't think it had anything to do with us. I thought it was on the other side of the estuary it was coming'. 'Well, we're not sure yet', he said, 'we're doing surveys to see which is the best option. Why I'm here is to show you where we're going to dig trial holes'.

So now, I thought, he's here to show me. I thought in my own mind if it was me that was in your shoes I'd be inclined to ask you. To ask permission from you first, at least. But he didn't. He said he was here to show me.

So I kind of played along with him. He talked out there for a while and took me down to the shed over there and the field over there from the house. That had been reclaimed and it had been reclaimed over a long time with a spade. It hadn't been level but a year before that we had ploughed it up and levelled it a bit. It was cut earlier in the year and the grass was growing back lovely and green in it. So he went over to the fence and said we'll be digging trial holes in there.

I didn't say yes or I didn't say no. Yeah, just in there, he said. We'll do no damage to it, he said. He said it's a good dry field. He said we'll be digging the trial holes with a JCB. Do you know what a JCB is, he asked? And he explained to me what it was! Well I didn't make him any the wiser that I knew or didn't know. And he said it's a yoke on wheels where you let down two arms when you're digging the holes. He said we won't damage the ground. Well, I said, I don't know about that. Ah well, he said, if you're not happy with that, we'll do it with a Hi-Mac. 'It's on tracks and that will do no damage'.

So at that stage I was getting kind of annoyed so I said it will definitely not do any damage. No, it will not, he said. I said that's the truth it won't because it won't go in there! With that he knew that I wasn't as innocent as he played me to be.

I said, do you think I'm childish or something. I said I know well what a JCB is and I know well what a Hi-Mac is. I guarantee you, I said, none of them will go in there. I told him 'you'll dig no trial hole in here'. And with that he left pretty fast that day.

MARY We had no notice at all from them that here was the pipeline route.

WILLIE He came back again then just asking how many of us were in the house. They'd come at a comical time when they'd figure you'd be busy. When the kids would be coming from school, that type of thing. They'd figure that you wouldn't have a great interest in them. He came then and he asked how many of us were in the house, whether there were any pylons on the land, any underground cables. A general survey. But at the same time he was kind of pushing you to sign – 'and then you'll sign here'. And he had handed you a biro.

MARY He'd be asking questions from the document – how many people, any pylons – and then he'd turn over the page. Now granted it might have been a general survey but as he was talking he'd say, 'and you can sign here'. Thank God for the sense of seeing through them. We'd ask, what are we to sign, can we see what we have to sign? 'Oh, I've only the one copy', he'd say. As you confronted him then he kind of backed out the door and moved on. The fear I had was how many did they do that to.

WILLIE He'd say then, well your neighbours signed.

WHAT WERE THE VIEWS AMONG YOUR NEIGHBOURS? WERE PEOPLE TALKING ABOUT THIS?

WILLIE Not really. They had local people picked as well to go around to the houses to say how good it was. That they were going to get money for nothing. The pipe was going to be put into your field. All that was said was that there was going to be gas in it but nothing was said about pressure. We didn't know anything about gas and pressure and that.

There were a few questions we asked ourselves. Why here, in bad boggy land? Why would I put so much hassle on myself as a big company with loads of money, why would I build a refinery where there's 30 feet of bog? It didn't make sense. Knowing what you can suffer in the bog. I knew what the bog was like. You have to be wary of it and you have to be careful. You keep as far away from it as possible.

MARY We started to hold meetings at this stage among a few of us. Monica and Gerard Muller were prominent at this stage. Gerard told me it would be the end of the place if it went through. After a while it grew. The One Voice meetings were going on as well. Others didn't want to get involved. They didn't want to know. We were focused on the whole project, not just the pipeline. But we had to concentrate at the beginning on the planning application for the refinery. That's really all we could have done. They didn't look for planning permission for the pipeline. Later on we applied to the Department of Marine about the pipeline and made submissions against it but it was all shrugged off. Minister Fahey took care of all that.

With hindsight maybe we focused too much on the planning process especially in believing that our own county council would actually turn against it. It was quite clear that they were happy to grant permission for this company. We thought – and we still do – that it should never have got planning permission. We found that the council had a very poor attitude. We focused on the planning because it was the only road to go at the time. There was no reason to focus on the pipeline at the time because if there was no refinery you wouldn't have the pipeline. That went on until October 2004 until they eventually got planning permission second time around from An Bord Pleanála. We did everything by the book. And this is not a 'terminal', as Shell describes it. You'd think it was at an airport. It sounds lovely. This is a refinery, the first in Ireland to be built on land with the waste emissions thrown out into our clean air.

WILLIE At that stage it was a complete change of life for the people. You'd go back the road and instead of talking to your neighbour you might see three men with a big jeep standing outside the door talking to him and telling him how good this was. You had to pass by that neighbour then rather than talk with him. You couldn't with them there. They went from door to door. The whole area was being changed. You could say that from 2000 until now that's all we have seen between Enterprise and Shell people. There have been jeeps and even helicopters which was something new to the area. That's what we have been looking at since.

But they wouldn't hold a public meeting where all the people would meet. These 'consultations' that they would have, they might start at two o'clock until eight in the college down there. The people would come at different times. I might go down there at two o'clock; my neighbour might go down at three. We wouldn't meet you see. They'd tell something different then to everybody.

MARY After a while we got wise and a few of us would go in together. We should be grateful we had enough sense to do things like that.

WILLIE You could sense from the image they were putting up that there was something wrong. When they didn't want to meet the people together, that was a sure sign that they wanted to divide them. That's the way it was.

MARY There were different reasons they got the percentage of people that did sign. Many signed because they saw that the Church was supporting it. Another percentage signed out of simply not asking the truth, accepting what they were told and not bothering to find out. Another percentage would have signed on the basis that it was equal to Bord Gais or to any gas pipeline in Ireland. We didn't know of anything else. Nobody in their wildest dreams could have believed that it could have been any different. When you add all that up that's how they got so many to sign.

WILLIE There was no word of pressure in the pipe. You'd meet a neighbour and he'd say, sure it couldn't be that bad. 'They'll put the pipe down and it'll be covered up again and you wouldn't see it in the field.'

Sort of out of sight, out of mind! They said that they were going to leave the land in a better shape than it was. That would-n't be such a big job around here because the land would be poor. They told people that they might seed the whole field for us. What they didn't tell them were the important things, much more important than covering a pipe in the ground and growing grass over it.

The One Voice meetings were a nightmare. We came home with high blood pressure and a sense that we'd be finished if this got in. The atmosphere was horrible. If you weren't for the gas you didn't exist. They didn't want you there. They gave us the impression that we were stupid, that we knew nothing. You'd put certain questions and rather than answer them they'd nearly tell you why are you asking.

MARY We were trying to get the local people to see why were they in favour and what were they focused on. Was their focus on what you'll get, what they'll give us – the crumbs off the table. We were being told that it was good for the area. We'll get this, that and the other. For example, we'll get a new set of jerseys for the local football team. Or we'll get a community centre.

WILLIE We were told that the local football club we were involved in would get everything, changing rooms, the lot.

MARY The reality is those kind of things don't exist. You can have all the community centres you like but unless you've a community to run them what good are they? Anyway, this company hadn't a notion of giving anything. I would come home from that meeting crying, not crying because I was weak, crying because I was so annoyed.

WILLIE I don't know what got into us, to give us the confidence to stand up. It's hard to pinpoint it. I saw harm in it from the word go. I don't know was it the fear of gas. I don't know if it was something like that that made us fear it.

I think it was the One Voice for Erris that sparked us off. We felt that these people were trying to downgrade us. They felt that we know nothing.

You looked at yourself and you'd say well I have to look at my end of the story. We figured where are the benefits as such. We were being told that there was going to be good. But when you asked the questions you wouldn't be answered. You kind of know when there are people beginning to pull the wool over your eyes. That's one thing I cannot stand for. You have to be straight and clean with somebody. You could see what was going on there. Also, it probably was the love of the land and the love of the place. We loved the place so much and we were both from the area.

The One Voice lasted four or five months. It lasted too long for us because it left us with sleepless nights. Coming home we'd be in a rage. You'd have these questions put forward and you'd have no answers got. We always kept nagging at them. We never let them go.

MARY If we had sleepless nights I'm sure they did too!

WILLIE We'd keep crossing them. The place would be up in an uproar nearly with shouting. At the very beginning there was only the two of us raising questions. I often came out of those meetings and I'd say we're not going through that again. I'm finishing with this tonight because I cannot take any more of it. And then lo and behold after you'd have the break got until the next week you'd say to yourself if I don't go to that tonight they're going to get away with it, what they're at. So you'd still go again. Maura Harrington joined us then which was a boost for us. It was one more who saw reality.

MARY The majority of the opinions at any of the meetings was the gas is coming. There was no such thing as it not coming. There were people asking questions about the environment, and how we have to look after the environment. But when it came to the planning for the refinery most of those people didn't put in a submission.

WILLIE At the One Voice meetings they'd tell us when we'd be getting on their nerves it doesn't matter what you think, the gas is going to come anyway. There's no way you can stop it coming when it is so big and there's so much money involved. You have to accept it. Try and get as much as we can out of it. As it went on you felt what are we at. Are we going against a brick wall? Our courage grew then and we got bolder and stronger. You tried to get your point across.

MARY The more we were put down the more determined we became.

WILLIE We used to think are we going too far with this? My father was sick at the time then and you'd have to be in and out of hospital. Taking the whole thing together you'd feel like lying down. But then you'd say to yourself if it's going to happen we're finished anyway. With this high pressure pipe outside your door. That quiet safe country life was finished anyway.

HOW DID YOUR KNOWLEDGE ABOUT THE PIPELINE GROW?

MARY We got together with others such as Gerard Muller and Micheál Ó Seighin and we got information at our own cost from the Internet and contacting people in other countries. You got no information from Enterprise. At their 'presentation days' if you asked one of them a question they'd say, 'oh I can't answer that, I'll put you on to the next guy.' And then that guy mightn't be there that day. You constantly got this. They never gave a straightforward answer. 'We'll take it away and have your answer the next day.' And at the next 'presentation day' the same thing. Nothing went in. It was just a one-way sound. We talked but they didn't listen.

WILLIE I had good knowledge of the ground. If you went down say two and a half metres into the ground there'd be dóib in it. And if it was touched it would start to boil and run. You lose complete control of it. I used say to myself sure they're going to go down over three metres. How could they do it? I used to picture them opening this trench through the village and going into this dóib and it just going out into the bay and everywhere. How were they going to control it? And I figured they didn't know how to control it either. We were guinea pigs. They were just trying something that was never done in the world before. That's what built our courage.

WHEN WERE THE COMPULSORY ACQUISITIONS?

MARY The first we heard was in November 2001. We could not understand how the Minister of the Marine was giving power to a private company over land. We felt his role finished at the high water mark. We always found that very hard to take in.

WILLIE Another thing that hit us was that we always figured that nobody can come into your land without permission. This was our experience going back for years with neighbours and boundaries and bogs. Your neighbour wouldn't come into your land and you wouldn't go into his to do something on it. I used to say how can they take our land without us consenting to it. Someone would say they can, they can take it for a road or for the ESB. Yet that was a different kind of a situation.

These weren't state bodies that were coming in to take your land. This was a multinational private company that was going to take your land. And a Minister of the Marine giving them permission to do it! You sat down at night and you thought to yourself there's something wrong here.

MARY Everything came in the post, right from the very beginning when they sent out the details of the pipeline route, the depth and the length of it. You had in the letter how much you were going to get per linear metre, which were crumbs. With that same letter it said you could get three pounds classed as early sign-up if you signed within twenty-one days. You were going to get three pounds extra for being a good boy or girl if you put your name to it! It also said in that same letter that it would save them having to go down the road of compulsory acquisition. They were threatening you in the same letter.

WILLIE The only really public meeting they had where the people were all together was when they were telling us about signing and what we were going to get. So much a linear metre and this type of thing. Then when the meeting was over they sat in different corners in the room and told people they'd give any information. But what the people really were doing was going to them to find out how much they were going to get.

MARY They had a land valuer with them. I remember someone phoning us up that night and saying have you been down with them? Did they tell you what you're going to get? That's how innocent they were. We didn't want anyone to make up what we were going to get. Looking back now, Enterprise Energy were more intelligent than Shell. As soon as they created a disaster they sold it off to Shell. Of course Shell thought they had got away with it.

WILLIE That's what went on. And people were delighted with that. Then when they were looking for the signing they told them it doesn't really matter whether you sign or not, there's compulsory acquisition anyway. But it would be more appropriate if you did sign to consent fully and you'd get your money faster.

I would have felt guilty if I was keeping our neighbours from getting €100,000. We were all good neighbours, everyone in the village. We helped each other over the years with no aggro. You'd say if my neighbour was getting €100,000 it would be a poor thing to be against him. But in fact the money was so small. We heard of these billions that Shell had yet they're giving us €6,000 or €7,000. This was a rip-off. So I didn't feel guilty for try-ing to stop it so that it could be done properly. I always said I'm keeping nothing from my neighbours anyway because they're getting nothing. They have sold themselves out for nothing.

When the Compulsory Acquisition Orders arrived we didn't know how we felt. I felt angry. I felt ready for a fight. Somebody coming in taking over our land, our father's lands, our great-grandfather's lands.

MARY The more you learned about it then the more you realised this just wasn't any ordinary story. As we understood Compulsory Acquisition this was the first for a private company. Compulsory Purchase Orders we were familiar with from the council and such. So now here's our country giving possession to a private company. It's not being purchased, it's just been acquired which means we will still have responsibility for it. Which was another fearful aspect of it. You just felt that if this private company can get this today it's a new line that can happen from now on in Ireland. Maybe not in the sense of gas or oil but there is an opening now for any private company to come in and acquire whatever they want. If this is let go ahead another company can come in and say that Shell or Enterprise got this down in Mayo so what's wrong with us getting it in Meath or Cork. It's a part of the Corrib gas issue people don't understand. For us, it's not just about stopping gas, it's not just looking for safety, there is a whole lot of sections to this. For anyone living in Ireland, their home or their land or their field can be obtained if the government decides tomorrow. They were trying to say it is in the national interest but that's not believable anymore.

WILLIE When you see someone starting to bully you to get something that really gets to you. If somebody wanted something off me and they go to bully me I'd just stick my heels in. You don't act that way. There's something wrong then at that stage when you ask questions and no answers but you get 'we're going to do it anyway'. When we did start keeping them off the land, the Shell man told me 'look it, we'll get it there anyway, regardless of what you're going to do'. That really gave you strength.

We started to read up on things at that stage and maybe listening to radio and listening to people who knew all about these things and getting information from other countries. Your mind was completely focused on it. That's what really sparked us off. Then to think that Fahey gave them permission at 9 o'clock on the night without going through the Oireachtas or anything. They changed the legislation to give them this CAO power at 9 o'clock on the night of a bank holiday weekend. It really was kind of suspicious I thought.

We had plenty of belief in the State up until this. But when this happened I said what are they doing to us? There they stand for us, you could say, being put out of our homes.

MARY It was hard to accept that our government was willing to let this happen. You'd feel that the government should be there to protect the citizens and they weren't doing it. They were helping out a multinational oil and gas company above ordinary Irish citizens. It's hard to accept that kind of thing. You'd feel like you shouldn't really have to put up a fight. We weren't only fighting the gas company we were fighting the government and even lower levels of the State such as the county council. As far as we are concerned they all played their part in the torture. It's nothing else but torture. Since 2000 it's been a silent torture. People had no idea the kind of things we were suffering and the kind of things we had to go through on a daily basis. Even if it was only a matter of having to go to the county council office in Castlebar, we had to travel 60 miles there just maybe to get three pages photocopied that we needed to prove that what we were saying was right. And pay for it! And return home and maybe have a meeting that night and then go about your ordinary daily life. All that was silent torture until the day the men went to jail. People in this country had no real idea of what we actually suffered as a small group and as individual people trying to get the truth out.

WILLIE And our kids knew that we were worried. We saw our kids going to school in the morning crying. One morning there was one of Enterprise's men had come in here at half eight in the morning. It was three days before they got their Christmas holidays. And the youngest girl cried all the way to school.

MARY She saw the kind of aggro that was going on between this guy saying that they were going to do it and us here saying no, you're not going to do it. These were the kind of days we had.

WILLIE The kids were listening to it quietly.

MARY Our families heard nothing but worry in our voices even during ordinary family talk when it should be the peak of some enjoyment. We went through christenings, we went through weddings, we went through funerals, all daily family things, we went through all of that as well as arguing about gas and trying to get answers about gas. I learned more in the last six years than I ever thought possible. There were times you'd get annoyed seeing other families enjoying life as though everything was normal, who would not, or could not, face reality for the future of our area if this company got its way.

WILLIE And we were isolated with little support. We had very little support until we went to jail. We had bits from different people who knew what was happening. The politicians ignored us completely.

MARY Michael Ring did help in a way but obviously he was called aside and told it's not party policy.

WILLIE They should have stood up for what we told them and the facts of how bad it was. And they know about it, they're not stupid. It sickens you to hear people knock Dr Jerry Cowley and saying he was jumping on the bandwagon of Shell to Sea to gain votes. Jerry didn't need us to get elected – he was already there.

WHAT WAS IT LIKE WHEN SHELL ENTERED YOUR FIELDS?

WILLIE Them coming on to the lands was hell altogether. They were coming on to mark a way for the pipe. When they'd come onto the land they would just turn up, no notice.

I was going through the village on the tractor one day and I saw two Shell people in my cousin's land. They had not sought permission. They were just in there stepping and measuring. But before I got as far as them they had left through the shore into the neighbour's field. I said to the headman that they were trespassing. 'No,' he said, 'we're not.' I said, 'two of your men were in there. That's what I call trespassing. You've no authority to be there.' 'We have authority.' I said, 'well if you have, show it to me.' He said, 'we don't need to show it to you.' I said, 'well we'll see about that.' I told him, 'don't come in again without showing me the permission you have.'

I came home then and I told Mary about Shell being in on the land. I went off then again and was about half an hour with one of the neighbours back here when Philip McGrath came as far as me and said that the guards were looking for me. That they were here at the house. Mary didn't know what had happened – did something happen to me on my way?

MARY The guards came here to the house and said how Willie wouldn't allow them into the field. They had been called by Shell. There were two of them there. I had never seen a Garda car ever come to our house. I said of course he wouldn't let them in because he hasn't seen the proof that they can do what they are saying. They said well we have seen it, they have shown it to us in the barracks this morning in Belmullet. In my naivety I said that's great. I was nearly relieved that they had this paper. We had been asking to see this for two years now. I said well would you mind giving us a copy of it. We don't have a copy, they said, they just showed the paper to us.

This paper was their version of the CAO which we had ourselves. Our argument was that they gained the compulsory acquisition without proper law and we knew therefore that what the guards had seen was what we had. But we were contesting whether that was lawful or valid.

It went from there then, one day after another. They obviously had made a complaint.

WILLIE They said I had abused them which I didn't, at any stage.

MARY We're quite used to Shell telling lies. It had got to the stage before the men went into jail that you didn't go out of the house without carrying a camera. Which was something we never had. I'd have loved to have a camcorder when my children were small to record true events of childhood that you'd want to look back on. We didn't want to have a camcorder to look at Shell. But you got to the stage when you had to because with the injunction they had taken out you didn't know what the injunction actually covered. [The preliminary injunction granted to Shell in April 2005 prevented named individuals and anyone from interfering in any way with any works undertaken by Shell.] Can you even look at them? The way they were acting and accusing us of things you'd have to have proof all the time.

WILLIE It was a nightmare at this stage. I told them at one point that I would go to jail if I have to. I always told them that. Fair warning. They laughed at me. You know this kind of smart remark, ah now will you go to jail, you wouldn't go that far.

MARY I mean one day in particular there was a piece on Mid-West Radio sometime in the morning, maybe half nine or ten. Andy Pyle the Managing Director of Shell was on. And he had this lovely spin saying about how they wanted to have dialogue with the farmers that had refused to sign and that they wanted to talk to them and that they couldn't progress with this kind of thing. Nice piece if you wanted to believe it. And that actual afternoon they were in on the fields in Rossport accompanied by the guards. So they had all this set up. While Pyle was putting this story out in the media for people who didn't live here and didn't know what was going on he was giving orders to his men to be on lands that afternoon and also had the guards. Even then, you couldn't believe what they were doing. He proved that that day. In rural Ireland if you call the guards it takes them awhile to be available. Naturally enough. We don't expect them to be sitting in their cars waiting for the first call. But they were in with them, funnily enough. So obviously they had to be notified earlier on that day so that two guards would be available plus a squad car. So they had it all set-up yet he still came out on the radio that morning.

WILLIE Different personnel of them came to the door several times telling us this and that and you'd ask them questions. But that wasn't their remit, they would say, it was somebody else's. Just to fob you off. We tried to get them to have a public meeting. We tried them several times to get the people together and have a public meeting. They would meet private, no problem, any time you wanted them. I'd say no, we'd better get this out in the open. But they'd never have a public meeting. Some of us who didn't sign up had planned questions when they visited. We all got different answers.

MARY They have turned around and said that the people here have stopped progress and they've held up the gas. But it's themselves that have done that not us. They created the situation that we are in now. They created the Environmental Impact Statements, they put them together. We had nothing to do with it. They are the ones that have made all the faults. They are the ones that have set the thing in our minds of not believing them. Every day that has gone by we have learned more. From programmes on Scotland and programmes on Nigeria, you name it. We weren't there, us five families, or anyone from Shell to Sea. We aren't living in those countries, we didn't do those things. I mean Shell can't deny that, they know these are facts. They know they're true. So how can anyone expect us to believe Shell?

WILLIE We know from all the information we have got that they're not going to treat us any different to what they did to the people of Scotland and Nigeria. That's the reality. What do you do then but to fight before it is too late. That's the way I look at it.

MARY There's too much proof of what they've created in other countries. But there is one thing that upsets me greatly. We have talked to people from Nigeria and they have told us that the Church supports people like us in their countries. You'd expect the same from our Church in Ireland.

WILLIE They have put this out in the media about us that we were only doing this to get more money. It is Shell that put out those spins. Money doesn't come into it which people should understand at this stage. They said we went to jail to get more money.

MARY But Shell would talk in those terms because to them money is the answer. Profit is all. People or environment doesn't come into the equation at all. Money for them is all and they'd nearly think how could it not be money. They can't understand the tie with the land and the ground and the community and your area. They don't understand that. We don't expect them to. But I do expect our government and the people who make decisions about our health to understand. Instead they're trying to push them through. Here we are celebrating the Land League and Michael Davit and 1916!

WILLIE There's a link there. It was fought for before to save the land. It's been fought for now again.

MARY As far as I'm aware Bertie Ahern is great into this community spirit thing. I think we even had a question on the Census Form about how much we participate in our communities. Well, we are protecting ours he'll be glad to know and without his help.

WILLIE If it was even our own resources you'd feel maybe we are stopping something. That we were keeping somebody from maybe getting a comfortable bed in a hospital. Maybe it might be myself that I'm keeping from it in years to come. I think it's terrible that the gas is gone and that there's no benefit from it. Everybody knows that it's not going to benefit the country as such because it's not ours.

And it's out there in our own waters! They're trying to bring it in through our own lands with all the destruction of it. And to think that we haven't a bit of claim to it! Well done political parties who support this!

HOW DID YOU REACT?

MARY One neighbour would tell another neighbour and we would all phone each other and the panic would start. I remember running out without breakfast on many mornings.

WILLIE There was fear among us at that stage. We got frightened. I used always tell my neighbours that they were going to put us to jail. Some would laugh at me, and say would you get a bit of sense.

You're making too much of a fuss about it. They won't put us to jail. I said, look you better be getting prepared because they will. There was something – I don't know what it was – I always knew they were going to go to the last straw. That didn't frighten me. I don't know what it was. I said right, if they're going to put us to jail, so be it.

MARY They actually did us a big favour in a way. Because it brought out into the open what really was happening. It brought the whole thing to a head. I don't know if they realise that it was the biggest mistake they ever made but for us it was the greatest thing they did for us.

WILLIE With hindsight we let them go with too much really. They brought all these caravans and portacabins to a field here in Rossport without planning permission. They put down a septic tank without planning permission which we had no right to let them do.

MARY They did that on the days we were out of the area when we were at the court in Dublin. I dare say they were watching every move we were making.

JUST BEFORE THE IMPRISONMENT THE CAMPAIGN SEEMED TO BE AT A LOW EBB?

WILLIE We were still going to battle it. We had made up our minds at that stage. I had even made up my mind that I was going to battle it on my own if need be. I told the guards and I told the whole lot of them that if it's down to myself and my family I'll be here. We had taken so much hassle from them. If somebody is going to do that to you without permission what would they do if they had gained permission and they had the better of us. The way I looked at it at that stage with all the information we had the only other choice we had left was to run away and leave.

MARY It was worth fighting for.

WILLIE As far as I'm concerned if it did come we would not live here. Even for your own good you would not live beside it with that pressure in the pipe and everything else. You'd be under mental torture all the time. So I said there is only one way – die now or die in ten years time from an explosion or from pollution. Mary had to be taken away for medical treatment one morning with exhaustion and stress.

MARY I ran too fast actually from breakfast to the field where they were coming in! It was pure fear. I actually felt at the time that Willie was up there on his own with them. This was more of the fear. He had spotted them.

WILLIE I was having breakfast at the table.

MARY Liam was on his way to school. He had said that the guards and Shell were gathered in one of the fields. God love him, he was on his way to do his Leaving Cert exam. This is what I mean by the torture. Imagine him going in and sitting his exam and thinking in the back of his mind that this was going on. I remember we were eating our breakfast and Willie had happened to look out the door and saw them going into the field above. He took off with the van. I was here. I was numb and I thought, oh my God he's up there and on his own with them. The fear that I had was that they would say he pushed them or hit them. We couldn't trust them. If I was there at least they'd be a witness. I ran out the door. It was teeming rain. What I actually did was I winded myself. I ran too fast and I wasn't able. And the fear. I just collapsed on the road. By the time I got there other men like Vincent and Ray Corduff had come.

WILLIE The sad part about it was when she collapsed they only laughed. That really got to me. I was holding her in my hands and their headman was smirking. He thought it was a put-on.

MARY I knew I wasn't sick – I had killed myself out. I knew I didn't really need any medical attention but everyone around me didn't know how bad I was. But at the end of the day I did go to the doctor. The doctor said that I was suffering stress and complete exhaustion. I thought that day and the next day could I keep this up. I don't know where we got the strength. This was about a fortnight before the imprisonment.

WILLIE I don't know how we did do it stress-wise. It was terribly emotional for us all the time especially coming up to the court. The only thing that did keep us going were the kids. 'Don't give in to them, Daddy.' When you hear your kids coming up to you crying and telling you 'don't give in' what can you do?

MARY They had learned so much about it. Every day of their lives from the last six years was taken with it. They knew as much as we did. They had grown up with it. They came out with us.

THE GOOD FRIDAY WALK IN 2005 SHOWED HOWEVER THAT THERE WAS SOMETHING HAPPENING WITHIN THE COMMUNITY?
(THIS WAS A SOLIDARITY WALK, WHICH STARTED AT THE CORDUFF'S FARM AND WALKED ALONG THE PIPELINE ROUTE TO THE PIER AT ROSSPORT.)

WILLIE That day was a reckoning for us. Mary used to say to me that the walk is going to be a disaster. It's going to show us up. She said there would be nobody at it. It'll show them that there's nobody behind us. I said to her no, I have a great feeling that the place is going to be mobbed. She said no way. But anyway come the morning we were up and waiting. It was slow to start. An odd one started to come. But when the walk was ready to start, it was massive. There were a good few hundred people there. That's really what set us off then.

THE MOOD WAS ALREADY BEGINNING TO CHANGE. WHY?

WILLIE The abuse they were giving us all.

MARY People had started to find out little bits. Things just didn't add up. It mightn't have been very significant but little things for people who had signed made them say now, hold on, I'm not happy about this. I think maybe that's why hundreds turned out that day.

WILLIE It was the community spirit too. The people knew us. They knew we never harmed anybody, that we were just quiet people who watched our own business. We had said to the community that we weren't trying to stop this but we were protecting everyone. We said there was loads of ways this project could have been done. They could have done it without bothering anybody.

It turned out that the community was listening even though you were getting the impression at times that you were wasting your time. But they were watching the wider picture, they were seeing what was happening to us. We were heard on local radio about what they were doing to us. Then there was the time they had planned to come in on the land the day my father was being buried. All that kind of thing got to the community. The walk showed the community we had. After the walk I used say to Mary, now are we on our own?

MARY About ten minutes before the walk started our first grandchild was born. Everything seemed to work. You'd say there is something that seems to send you on the right path.

WILLIE The change among the people was happening.

THEN THERE WAS THE LORRY BLOCK?
(THIS OCCURRED WHEN A LORRY SERVICING SHELL'S WORK COMPOUND IN ROSSPORT WAS UNABLE TO TRAVEL PAST A LOCAL CAR ON THE NARROW ROAD INTO THE VILLAGE. LOCAL PEOPLE REFUSED TO REMOVE THEIR CARS TO ALLOW THE LORRY PASS.)

WILLIE When the lorry was blocked the people did come out.

MARY Again Shell did try and say that we blocked it. There was no talk about the reality that the actual road into our village was too narrow and that they couldn't be bothered setting up a plan to widen the road and spend money on it. They and Mayo County Council thought they could just use the road and we would stay back and stay at home.

WILLIE The guards told us to shift our vehicles and let them through. It's you that's blocking the road, they said. But this lorry was the full width of the road! We were in as far as we could go. And yet the guard came up to us and told us to move. To clear the way for Shell.

MARY They could never see the point that we were trying to make that an accident could easily happen along that road. A lorry could turn over on that road as quick as a click of your fingers. They could never see that we were at a cut-off point if anything happened on that road. There was no other access for this village because we had only the one road out of it. What if there was an emergency? We of anyone knew how important it was to get a fire brigade quickly here or an ambulance or anything else. That was the point we were trying to make. All Shell and the county council had to do was spend the money. You'd blame the county council more than Shell because it was up to them to look after our roads and make sure it was wide enough for both vehicles to pass. But of course we had to take the brunt of it and take the blame.

DID THE LORRY INCIDENT GAVE PEOPLE A WAY OF OPENLY CONFRONTING SHELL?

WILLIE They said we had deliberately blocked the lorry. What happened was we were getting fed up with having to reverse back. We had done that for a good while. We did meet lorries before that and we did reverse back into the crossroads again to let them in. A lot of people were doing that and they weren't saying anything about it. Vincent McGrath met the lorry on the road. He just pulled up and in all fairness he was well in on the side. Then some other car came behind him and some other and it built up from that. We were actually in Killala that day on the way home from one of the courts. The guards could see for themselves that the road was incapable of carrying big lorries. It was a total destruction to a small community if there was an accident with one road out of the area. You just couldn't imagine it.

MARY It was the sort of disregard they had for the people and the area where they didn't even think it worthwhile to spend the few euros on re-widening it.

WILLIE If they did build a fine road in there at the beginning we'd probably have sat back and let them do what they were going to do. But they didn't even make an effort.

MARY They were talking about giving things to the community. If they didn't even think it worthwhile to keep that community safe during the process of putting in the pipeline obviously they would have no regard for anything.

WILLIE We had run-ins with them before with their jeeps. The worst part of it was people thought that it was us that was doing it deliberately. That used to get to me. Shell contractors used to cross the road in front of us with their jeeps. To frighten us. Things happened that people wouldn't believe to this day happened. I had three incidents myself with one Shell person. With two of them I was driving alone. The third one Mary was with me. You couldn't go reporting it because they'd only laugh at you. It was at that stage that Mary said we'd have to get a camcorder. The day she was with me we were going to Ballina. At Belderrig a senior Shell man was driving towards us. The next thing he drove straight across in front of me. Only that she was with me she'd nearly have asked me later did he do it. She would not believe he would do that.

MARY This is the disregard they had. If you go back to the time they were coming in when Willie's father had died, okay, they sent us a condolence letter as those kinds of people do. But about three weeks later a letter came out in the post telling Francis Corduff what they'd be doing in the next few weeks. They send out a condolence letter when you're dead and the next thing they send this. They didn't even look up to see who they were writing to.

WILLIE People don't realise the awful time we had with them. With my father sick everything was so hard to do. It all probably hardened us up. The fire we had before that probably hardened us up as well.

COURT - THE DAY OF THE COMMITTAL

WILLIE We knew we were heading for jail. We didn't know what jail was like. We didn't know if you could bring clothes in with you. We didn't know what it was. We hadn't a clue. She said, I'd better pack a bag for you. But I didn't bring it. I said no, I'm not making anything easy for them. If I have to go to jail I'll go to jail in these clothes. She'd be saying, oh God they're not going to put you to jail. I'd say I've a funny feeling they will. But until reality hit, I was saying they are going to put us to jail but at the back of my mind I was saying no. I was preparing myself for something that was not going to happen. But it happened. It was terrible.

MARY We did see a memo where Shell had debated – Andy Pyle and his PR people – whether they should have us all committed. It was in that memo that they actually said it would make bad publicity. So they decided to single out a few then.

WILLIE It was the most awful thing that ever happened to me. I never will forget it. It was horrific. To leave your wife and family. I mean we were never apart before. Jesus, I thought, here goes, this is it now. The fearful part was how long were we going to be there.

We had talked a lot about it – it shows what we used to talk about – before we went to jail. Even the neighbours used to say to each other – someone of them would tell me – they'll take Willie and throw him in jail and continue with the work. They would say to me, that's what they're going to do to you and don't be silly, you have to think of your family. I used answer well I am thinking of my family, that's why I'm doing it. My family is behind me. They'd say, if you are put to jail and left there what's going to happen? So I said those are the consequences we have to take. Even the night before the court Mary was saying you'll be put to jail and that'll be it and you'll be left there for God knows how long. Well, I said, if they do, we'll have to just wait and see what's going to happen.

But the day we were put to jail it was devastating. It was frightening. We hadn't a clue what we were facing. We were brought from the Bridewell to Mountjoy in a dark van without room for movement. We were each caged separately in the van. It was as dark as a confessional box. It was frightening to be in there not knowing what was going to happen. We didn't know whether we were going to be together. We didn't know what was the situation. There was only one thing I had in my mind – whatever the consequences we were going to stick it. I wasn't going to give in. If the other four broke I think I'd still stick it. This determination was in my mind. It's going to take whatever it's going to take. You'd think of the kids then, you'd think of Mary, you'd say am I doing right or am I doing wrong? You could feel like it was the finish of you, the ruination of you. We were moved later that evening to Cloverhill prison, which was to be our address for the next ninety-four days.

Then when we got brought in and settled in the first day we knew there was going to be three of us in the one cell and two in the other. At least that was something. We didn't know whether we were going to meet, we didn't know whether we were going to be let out in the morning, or are we going to be in here all the time. It was terrible.

I mistrusted the court from day one. I was never in court in my life. I never knew anything about courts. I never knew how they worked. We had different legal teams at different times. What they did to us I will never forget until the day I die. It will always be on my mind. All they wanted was for us to take compensation. I had told them from day one that it wasn't a money issue. 'If you're going to fight it fight it for us. Don't be thinking that it is for money that we're doing it.' They'd still come back and tell you that it's the easiest way out of it. You should seek for a big lump off them, they'd say. That used to kill me because it wasn't about money. As I always said we weren't used to money. We managed without money. This wasn't going to change. Even though I had said if they gave me ten million I wasn't going to take it. And I needed it badly! But it was never about money.

It had taken the court four and a half days to give Shell the injunction. We had been talking to people in the hall and everyone had told us that if you're going in for an injunction it will only be half an hour. You'd either get an injunction in half an hour or ten minutes, either yes or no. I used to say when the day would go by what's wrong here. How come ours is lasting? And then on the day Judge Finnegan gave it to them he said I'm giving it to you but I don't know whether I'm doing right or wrong. And I'm giving you permission to install the pipe. And if it's proven in the courts that it's wrong I'll make you take it up again. I won't let you put gas in it.

I had the cop-on to know that if they do get the pipe in, that's us gone. That's it over. The gas would go into it then, they'd never take it out. We had no representation at the committal hearing. We were on our own. Finnegan asked Micheál have you got a family car, have you got a home. He said I can take all that off you. He meant us all. I can take all that off you and I can fine you hundreds and hundreds of thousands and I'll find a way that you will pay it. And I'll take the land of every farmer in Mayo if I have to.

I said, my God, is this real? Frightening and all as it was. He said then I'm giving you ten minutes to go out and talk it over to see the consequences of what you're doing. At that stage I turned over to Philip beside me and I said he cannot take blood out of a stone. Even at that frightening stage I was looking up at him and I thought don't try and frighten me. You could see he was trying to frighten us. That's what was in my mind. It made me stronger in fact to see what he was trying to do. After the sentence I turned around and there was a local journalist crying. It made me ask myself was I all right? That's what got to me really. It was real. And there were tears all around in people. I thought is this real or am I gone out too far? It was frightening.

It was bad for about two days for us. The two full days weren't up when we started to get reports back about what our families saw when they got home. That's what really brought us back again. The way I describe prison was that it was like catching a fox and putting him into a dog's cage. Or catching young wild ducks and penning them in along with the tame ducks. It was a completely different life for us. We were used to freedom. I used to say to Micheál – he would still laugh about it – I'd say it was about the third day when we were coming back to ourselves – I said to him out in the yard, you're okay.

He looked at me and said what are you on about? I said, this is no change for you and Vincent. You got up in the morning at eight, and you went into the college at nine o'clock. You were then imprisoned until four.

You came home and you ate or whatever and then went into a room and stayed there until you went to bed! He thought this was hilarious.

He said, I suppose you have a point. I often got up in the morning at half six and I might not get back in until the evening. I even ate outside many times.

I don't know how I managed it. But after two days I did manage it. Once we heard about the support. The first thing Mary said on the telephone was to hang in there because the support is there. As soon as I got a sense of what was happening on the ground I was happy because I figured now we're not on our own.

MARY I'd say not a day went by that some television station didn't cover something on the Corrib gas and on what was happening. The time of isolation was over, now the country was hearing the story of Rossport and the abuse of the gas company on a small community and the neglect of the government to protect us.

WILLIE We would listen to the radio and the television and we could see what was happening. When Mary told me about the people protesting locally I asked how many were there – twenty or thirty. She said, there are hundreds! They're from everywhere. They're calling to the house and ringing. Well, I said, this is it. Let them keep us here if they want. Then the word came about the third day that they have pickets at Ballinaboy and that all Shell work has been forced to stop. The people of the community came together and probably saw for the first time how Shell really operates.

MARY They knew then that they had done the right thing in going to jail. Regardless of what length they'd be in. It was hard, very hard but they knew they had taken the right step.

WHAT WAS PRISON ROUTINE LIKE?

WILLIE The warders started to wake people up soon after six when they opened one of the locks on the doors and looked in. There was a television there and an electric kettle. You could make tea for yourself. We were nearly full-time drinking tea to pass the time! The toilet was in the same room. You went down for your breakfast before nine o'clock and queued with your tray to get your cereal. You brought it back to your cell then. You were there until about ten when you'd be let out into the yard. You could be let out earlier for your shower or to go to the shop. Then you met all different types of people in there for all different types of crime.

MARY Everyone in there supported them because of the reasons they went to jail.

WILLIE The first time we went out into the yard with the other prisoners we didn't know anything. We didn't know what was going to happen. There were some people there with drug problems and drink problems and all sorts of problems.

MARY People that society had let down.

WILLIE We wondered were we going to be all right. It opened my eyes. I never will forget it. We didn't know that that kind of thing was happening. I mean we'd get up in the morning at home and do our jobs and you wouldn't think of anything like that. Ever since prison it never leaves my mind. I had family myself, I had sons at the age of those lads in there, and I thought they belonged to some father and mother too. Society had let them down. They had nothing to do but steal. Putting them in jail wasn't going to correct them. It was going to ruin them. That's what I felt. If they were put somewhere where they could do something and be given some training. The majority of them were okay, they just needed someone to direct them.

We stuck out a mile. I mean we weren't for there at all. We were the oldest that was there, they were nearly all young. 'What are you in for?' You'd tell them and they'd say, no, no, will you stop that. You must have given them a good hammering! Then another fellow would stick his head in and say, sure the land

mustn't be belonging to you at all! You must be trying to take
it over from other people. Not until they started watching
television that they realised that we were telling them the truth.
Because no way would they believe us. Because we couldn't be
in jail they thought for trying to keep somebody off your own
property. At night then when the marches would come on the
television we'd be watching it and you'd hear the cell doors
being banged and kicked and shouting showing support for us.

The warders told us at the beginning that we'd be under the
same regime as the other prisoners. We weren't treated any
differently to any other prisoner nor did we expect to be. We did
the same schedules they had. We queued up for our lunch and
our dinner and whatever. We were allowed to make a six-minute
phone call each day. We were not allowed a watch, money or any
of our own possessions.

Certainly, there were nights we went in to our cells and said
right, this is it, we won't stay here much longer, we cannot. But
we were 94 days in there and we didn't think we were thirteen.
We couldn't believe it was September. We used to say where is
the time gone. Then we used to feel about those outside are we
selfish with the torture they're going through. Our families used
to land in Dublin looking worn-out. I would come to the glass
and see Mary and say I'd better get out of here because she's
going to be dead. She used be wrecked looking. I said, is it
really worth it but she always encouraged me that it would be.
The worst part of it was with their journey up and down. I used
to worry was something going to happen to them. With all the
accidents on the road. I'd lie in bed at night and say, I'll
probably regret this because she'll get killed or they'll have a
crash. Because they were on the road so much. We didn't know
how they got home. You'd listen to the radio at night and you'd
hear there was a car accident in Kinnegad. You didn't know was
it them. You thought you'd hear in the morning that they're in
hospital or they've had a bad crash. It was a nightmare.

You'd see the kids coming in crying, you'd see the tears in
their eyes sometimes, they weren't able to talk. Our son Francis
came home from England the night I went in to the prison. You'd
think then is it going to do them harm. They were youngsters
and hot-tempered and I'd worry would he go down there and do
something out of the way from sheer stress and anxiety.

The glass was terrible. When you visit Cloverhill you can only talk through a glass window. You are separated. There is no physical contact. It was cruel.

MARY The way it's designed the sound is carried under you and you're trying to make eye contact with the person inside. You're nearly lying sideways. You also had the sound of other people around. In there your voice was lost. The longer the visit went on or the later your visit, the more crowded it would become. But the other prisoners along the screen would be waving at us and saying, fair play to you. It would give you a lift.

WILLIE The other prisoners were used to this. The majority of them were in and out. It was a way of life for them. Mary used to come sometimes and say that they'd been waiting outside for an hour and a half. That used to kill us yet you had to keep the bright side out. You had to give the impression that you were sound.

MARY You left sometimes from Rossport at four or five in the morning to arrive for the early visit.

WILLIE You couldn't get emotional. You had to keep all that inside you. You also were aware that you couldn't really talk. Especially when you'd see them going. You'd kind of say to yourself am I all right? You'd say, am I putting too much effort into this, is it as bad that I have to do this for it? Then, when you'd go back into the cell again and you'd watch something about Shell on television that night you'd be away again. You'd take another day out of it.

MARY But as bad and all as it was, and it was very bad, you still had it in your mind that Shell would be worse. That Shell would treat you worse than prison. It's a sad thing that you have to compare. Any other person would say the thought of three months in jail would be the end of you. But you had to put it in the context of how bad it would be if Shell got in here.

WILLIE The hardest day I had in there was the day that Bobby Peek from South Africa came in to visit. I had to stop talking to him. He kept talking about my son Liam. That day really took me down an awful lot. He started telling me about how devoted

Liam was to what he was doing on the farm, how hard he was working. I knew that myself. You'd say to yourself, should I not have been out there with him? There were some terrible days. Days we'd go back to the cell and there'd be crying. There's no point saying it didn't happen. We cried ourselves to sleep. It was a great thing that the three of us were together at least. We were lucky that we did get over it. After we came out though you could tell it had an effect. Before this if you heard of someone going to jail you wouldn't even think of it the following day.

MARY It's one thing being in jail and caught and put through court and found guilty of what you're there for but in the men's eyes and most people's eyes they were put to jail for something you shouldn't have been in jail for.

WILLIE If you were put in there for doing something you'd have a job to deal with prison.

MARY You'd say, well this is the punishment. I have to deal with the consequences. But the way the men went to jail they felt like they should not have been there.

WILLIE Even out in the yard I used be cracking jokes and saying the next time I'll be in jail I'll be in for doing something! But there were several people in there that were innocent. That's the sad part of it. And there were people who deserved to be there. They'd admit it themselves. They used to say to us we're in here but we don't mind, we're in for a reason.

MARY They became a number. Their number would be called out for visits or lunchtime or to make a phone call. They weren't known by their name.

WILLIE There were times you'd enjoy some of it. We used to be entertained at the banter the prisoners would give the warders.

MARY The visits were a frightening experience for us as well. When you went up to reception you got a number. If someone had been there that day on a visit that you didn't know then you lost your visit. They only got one visit a day. It was hard to imagine that that could happen. We used to be so afraid going up to Dublin that someone would have used up your visit. Then you'd give in the name and get your card and be called with that number on it. The process would take so long. Then you got that and went out into the yard and across to the entry door. I think there was about three sets of locked doors to go through to get into what was still a locked area. We had no contact with them. There was a glass screen between us. That was very difficult. I remember one day in particular Enda Kenny was there on a visit. The one thing that broke my heart was to know that Enda Kenny was going to have a visit in the same room with them. Here we were looking in through a glass at our husbands and we couldn't touch them. That used to kill me. I thought it was so unfair. I have heard of Enda Kenny's experience of how he was mugged somewhere in the past and how he had described the awful, lingering sound of the knife being taken from its holder. I could describe the awful sound of the keys locking and unlocking the gates and doors as we waited. The feeling of helplessness overcomes you.

However, the politicians going in did them good! I remember going up another day and Willie was in the best form. They had had a visit from Enda Kenny and his friends. It sparked them. It made them angry. The anger kept them going in prison. It kept them going a lot of the time. Anger at the politicians, anger at Shell.

WILLIE The visits were a laugh with some of the politicians. I couldn't just hold back. I had to just let fly. The thing was we were in there. The thing that used to kill me was we were put in there for protecting ourselves, our homes and our families. I thought that was terrible. That was the most thing I couldn't take. It was putting us out of our homes. Where do you go then?

MARY Our background would have been Fianna Fáil supporters. That was even harder to take. You'd be ashamed to say that that was the party your father and mother and the generations before you had supported.

WILLIE I was never the one for politics. I'd never pay much heed. My father and mother and all their people were Fianna Fáil. We thought it was the right thing. That's what you followed up. But you'd be so ashamed now to think how you were led astray.

Other than one local councillor no Fianna Fáil politician came in to see us. I couldn't believe it. That's what used to vex me when it was said that it was a Sinn Féin-planned campaign. That wasn't right. They were one of the parties that did give us support. At least they were there. We'd have given the same reception to Fianna Fáil or Fine Gael. We drew no line on any party who supported us.

MARY You had support at grassroots level but because it wasn't party policy they couldn't act on it. It's sad that that's how our country has gone.

WILLIE Even going back a few years I had copped myself on and I had decided that I wasn't going to vote at election time. My father would say are you not going down voting? I used say can you tell me who I should vote for? You'd see the corruption that was going on at that stage, even before the gas. On the day of the election we would nearly not speak and that wouldn't happen very often because we were very close. The only arguments we used ever have were on election day! You'd be ashamed now to think of what Fianna Fáil did to us. My people were very strong Fianna Fáil people.

THE RELEASE?

WILLIE We had no sense the release was coming. Even the day we were released we were full sure that we were back in again. I was sure we were going back to prison. But at that stage I don't think we cared. We were going to go back in if necessary.

MARY Maybe we should have asked Shell on the day to drop continuing the injunction case against the men.

WILLIE Shell and the government got away too lightly on our release. I suppose we were so delighted to think it was coming to an end at that stage. However, we couldn't apologise for what we had done. We had done nothing out of the way. We couldn't apologise for something we didn't do.

We didn't set out to beat Justice Finnegan. We didn't set out to put anyone down, either the government or Finnegan. They created the situation for us. They wanted to put us down if we had allowed them. I hate to be put down in the wrong. I was always like that. If somebody put me down in the wrong I'd never give in to them. If I had done something wrong I'd be the first one to come and say I'm sorry, it's my fault. But I just can't bear to have someone accuse me in the wrong. It was the same with the jail. I don't doubt I'd be there forever if I had to apologise. I couldn't do it. You couldn't just go in front of Finnegan and tell him you were sorry. For what? For protecting yourself? It couldn't be done.

MARY You'd think back over these things and you'd say the intention of the system was that they'd be out in 24 hours. That the most it would be would be a week. You'd know that's what they hoped. They never expected that it would go on for three months, that the men would stick it out that length. Shell never thought they'd go to jail.

We used to laugh at the guards with the doors all locked. We used to make a joke that they could leave the doors wide open and those fellows have no notion of coming out. They could leave the key with them!

During the summer there were some nights you got to bed at two or three o'clock in the morning. You were on the road again at six – three hours' sleep some nights. There were days you were so exhausted you could hardly talk.

There were no regular dinner times or hours. I remember one day in particular we had dinner here at the house. I remember thinking to myself, thank God we're having dinner today. Those sort of things that we didn't have. There were times when neighbours and friends cooked pots of stew and casseroles for us. They were so kind.

We were thrown into the media. I wouldn't say we were well able for it but we did our best. For me to talk to a camera was very difficult. You had to watch everything you said. You didn't always know what to say or what was the right thing to say.

You didn't know how people who were listening would regard you. Would they think that you were just looking for attention? In all fairness I have to say that the media treated us pretty well. There were only a few exceptions. For us, it was a matter of telling the truth. That's all we knew so we didn't need rehearsal for that.

WILLIE You wouldn't care but she hadn't the gift of the gab! She was quiet and quiet-spoken. She wouldn't be one to get involved or giving out. She's quiet.

MARY You had to. But it was a different world.

WILLIE It was a good thing that it was me that was put in and not her. It was far harder on them than it was on us.

MARY You were always in the public eye even if you were in some street in Dublin or Cork or Cavan. I travelled counties in this country I had never been in. The support that you met with then kept you going for the next event. Along with that you had to deal with everyday chores and family life. It was a nightmare really.

WILLIE You had your family all out there in the public eye. Otherwise we wouldn't be known about.

MARY It was hard. We used to get upset after going to Dublin. You'd have to try and be strong. It was very hard sometimes. The phone too was unbelievable. I remember about a week after they were jailed, I had a terrible earache. I know myself it was because of the mobile phone. It was constantly at my ear. I wouldn't have used the mobile before this thing bar the odd time. But you were constantly on it.

There were some days that you just couldn't take any more of it, it was so bad. But it worked out all right. It was a terrible experience. There were highs and lows. Each day that passed of the ninety-four days there was more support – Irish support and international. It grew and grew and that made you stronger. We got letters and cards from all over. There were ones we got that might be signed 'old school friend' or 'met you sometime', or 'thanks for standing up for us and protecting our future.'

WILLIE The post was one thing that kept us going in prison. We got letters and cards from all over the world supporting us.

MARY One woman in particular who wrote had stayed with us as a student in the Gaeltacht. She saw the name on the paper and said it had to be us. Then she just wrote after not having contacting us in twenty or thirty years. Those things meant the

world to us when we got such backing and support.
I was going a day at a time for the first while of it. During the
first week of the imprisonment the Dáil went on holidays. The
end of August was probably the hardest time because I thought
the Dáil won't be back until the end of September and that
nothing much would happen until then. Up to that you thought
something might happen. Foolish of me. One of the most
annoying things looking back was that hardly a day went by
without Andy Pyle or someone from Shell saying they couldn't
lift the injunction.

They did it on every statement they put out, they did it on
every interview – television, papers and radio – they couldn't lift
the injunction. We heard him say on The Late Late Show when
we were all on that they cannot lift the injunction. And then, lo
and behold, they could lift the injunction when it suited them.
And they expect us now to have faith in what they tell us? They
expect us now to have confidence in them. By jailing our
husbands for ninety-four days, by telling us they couldn't lift
the injunction, by their histories in other countries, they expect
us to have faith in them? How could we? If Shell told me
tomorrow that they had changed their mind and that they were
bringing a water pipe now to Rossport I wouldn't believe them.
I'd be terrified of them. That's a fact. From the experience we've
had of them.

WILLIE There's no way back for Shell in this area. Even if it was
only myself I will never give in to them. Never. Regardless of
what the consequences are going to be I'm not going to give in
to Shell. Because you couldn't after seeing what they have done
all over the world. It would be the end of our life if they did get
in. You might as well end it now as end it then.

MARY Had we been living in a country that allowed hanging
would Shell have asked for them to be hanged? That's the
reality of it. They went as high as they could go in Ireland to the
High Court. Of course, there was no need to bring us all the way
to the High Court in Dublin. That was convenient for them, for
their solicitors and their offices. We were inconvenienced in
every way possible. They had money and had access to
everything in Dublin. Yet they hauled us from the West of
Ireland all the way to Dublin to defend ourselves.

WILLIE There's no point in saying we haven't bitterness. We have and we will forever.

MARY You can't just forget last summer.

WILLIE If a neighbour had put me to jail over a dispute we'd never see eye to eye again. I don't think you can get anybody civilised that would put you to jail over an argument.

You might half forgive them but you're never going to forget. Somebody that put you away from your wife and family? If I had killed someone or harmed someone and was put to jail I might forgive them then. But I only ever wanted to get answers from them.

MARY You asked questions and you were jailed.

WILLIE That will never leave my mind. It will never leave the family's mind. Our families feel bitter to them.

MARY They use words like 'we'll move on', it was 'regrettable' what we did last summer, Shell has 'learned lessons'. What lessons have they learned? Nothing. Let them prove to us the lessons they have learned. I don't think they've learned any lesson.

WILLIE It was the people of the country that got us out of jail with their support. Only for that we would still be in jail. But for the community they'd put us back in again but they're afraid. They'd have us back there tomorrow morning if they could get people to stay away from us. And they'd leave us there and do their work. That's what I find about Shell. They're arrogant.

MARY They've come out with several statements about how it was regrettable and we need to move on. At the same time they're appearing in the locality, going door to door, talking to people. They are still there trying to aggravate you. They still haven't learned.

WILLIE The only reason they agreed to mediation was to get us out of jail. They're not prepared to mediate about anything. What have they changed since we got out of jail? Absolutely nothing to do with the project apart from the company changing their personnel. They seem to think if they remove the staff who were around when we were jailed that we might forget the past. Move them on to some other country to abuse some other community.

MARY You wouldn't wish on your worst enemy the project that they've planned.

WILLIE That's why they cannot move from here because they have nowhere to go. Nobody wants them. People come up to me and say would it not have been easier to take money from them than going to jail. But when you turn it around and say, right if it was you, would you take money and leave your home, they wouldn't. That's the reality of it. I cannot see anybody that would want it outside their front door. Shell knows that too. As far as I'm concerned if Shell cannot succeed here that's them finished. That's why they're going to press hard here.

MARY We've made a lot of new friends from the whole thing. There are a lot of concerned people in this country. About many issues.

HOW DO YOU FEEL ABOUT BEING PUBLIC FIGURES?

WILLIE We're trying not to recognise that we are! It's tough being thought of as a 'hero' for people who don't want that. There are people who would love to be heroes. They'd enjoy it. But we never set out to be heroes. And I don't want anyone ever to class me as a hero. I don't class myself as a hero. We just did something that I know was right. I don't want to be classed as a hero for it. I just hope that it will finish by us getting back to the way we were.

MARY It would be nicer though to have something written in history about being a hero than have something written about being in a disaster.

WILLIE There's no point in closing the door when the horse is gone. God forbid if one half of the village did blow up and the other half survived there was no point in us saying then why

didn't we do something. If we had known the risk in advance.
You'd feel terrible. I would. If that did happen and you were left,
you'd never forgive yourself. To say I knew it all along, I was told
it by people, I was given all the information and I just sat down
and ignored it hoping it would never happen or hoping someone
else would deal with it.

MARY There were often moments in low times when you'd say
I wish I was like those people that can't see the harm in it. It
would have been much easier for us. We wouldn't have had to go
through all this torture. But when you see that it is wrong you
just cannot not act.

WILLIE It has changed our view of Ireland too.

MARY Has the standard that's been applied to this project been
applied to others? You'd wonder is there anything done right in
this country. It's frightening.

WILLIE You'd ask yourself sometimes am I in Ireland? It's not
the Ireland we used to know. I always thought that companies
and government would abide by law and that everything was
done fairly straight. But look at all the crookedness we have
seen since this began. We heard about things happening in
Nigeria and so on but we always heard there was no law in those
countries. But we have it here in Ireland. It's not the Ireland we
were brought up in.

MARY It has made us aware of the wealth that's out there off
our coast. All that's going to be done for us is that we're going
to be used for access and then it will be sent off to benefit other
countries. Even Norway is getting a percentage of this. We can't
gain one cent from it. You just wonder what kind of mind-frame
would be on someone to give that kind of gift away. I know the
Irish were always classed as a generous people and friendly and
easy-going but there's a limit to friendship! You can't give
everything away for nothing.

CHAPTER 2

'What worried us all the time was that there was nobody asking questions'

Micheál and Caitlín Ó Seighin

BACKGROUND

MICHEÁL The first time I came here was with a bunch of graduates from Galway in June 1962. It was a gorgeous weekend. I had taken the job at that stage in the secondary school in Rossport. It was just a tiny secondary school run by Gael Linn. At the time I was Tánaiste of Comhchaidreamh (The Society of Irish Speaking Graduates) who had established Gael Linn some years before. I had volunteered to come here as a teacher. At the time there was a great difficulty in getting teachers for here for all sorts of reasons. So I volunteered, intending to stay for two years. I came therefore for two years and I've been here since! There wasn't any reason to leave. And the strange thing was that there are quite a number of men from my own area, which was high in the mountains in east Limerick, who married girls from this area. Many did so in England. So there was an empathy with the place unknown to myself. I found it easy to fit into the place.

CAITLÍN I was born and reared here up the road from where we now live. I have lived all my life here apart from two years when I taught in Bangor Erris and in Dublin. I came back to Ceathrú

Thaidgh to finish research work that I had been doing on local phonetics with An tAth Colmán Ó hUallacháin. I met Micheál and I didn't leave again! We married and settled down here.

I just love the place, the history of it, the people, the songs, the stories and the way of life here in Dún Chaocháin. When I was growing up we were full of stories about our own area in particular. It was a poor enough time of course. People had to go to England. But I love the whole area and everything connected with it.

MICHEÁL A friend of mine from Cork used to say to me that he wouldn't need a car if he was painting here. He could spend all his time painting in the one spot, he said. I could understand that though I remember saying to him early on that there must be very little colour because of the bleakness of the area. He said no, in fact the light makes up for any lack of variety. The light, the overall colour, is constantly changing. He said that he could paint the same thing, like water lilies, over and over and I'd still be on the surface, he said, because all I'd be doing is painting what you could see on the outside. But I would have no shortage of subject matter.

Maybe he had hit on something faster than people normally would. There is a means of connecting with this place through the Irish language. I'm sure this is the case throughout the country. You also had it in my own place. I could understand it from my mother before the remains, the echoes, of the Irish language disappeared. With Irish the entire area is a unity, whereby the place where things happen becomes part of the event itself. So the placenames become a record of any particular event. You have got milestones in the place for any story whether it is something that happened to me recently or something that happened a hundred years ago. You have these indicators in the place all the time. In telling anecdotes you find yourself spatially establishing them all the time. Place seems to give credibility to the experiences of the people. As a language that is not borrowed but indigenous, its idioms and dialect difference have been honed to represent and describe a world always changing which has the effect of tying the people and the area together.

I find it shocking now to hear people in areas where Irish is declining, even in Rossport, where for example many of the young people don't know where the carraig dhubh is. The Carraig Dhubh is a very important rock, an indicator, to keep a boat coming in from the rocks. If you don't know where the carraig dhubh is then there is an element of the economic survival of the area that you don't have.

There is a unity of experience in the language. You need those codes to understand the area. Differences in dialect seem to reflect differences in the origin of population, even in various parts of Erris which hasn't a particularly big population. You do need to know that there are different nuances, different ways of seeing reality that different parts of the area have. It is very important to know this. The people realise that.

I remember the first evening I was in Rossport in 1962. I was staying in the house of Anthony John (who died a year afterwards), a wonderful, remarkable man. He took me for a walk and I didn't know at the time why. He took me along to the shore and around the sweep that is Rossport and back along the other side. He was pointing out the houses to me and saying 'my uncle is there', 'my first cousin is there' and 'that man up there is my relative'. I was young but by the time I had ended the walk I had known exactly what Anthony was doing. What Anthony was saying to me was keep your mouth shut until you know where you're going and everything will be okay.

The whole area is looking to the sea rather than looking to land. But even within Erris there are distinctions between one part of the area and another. You would engage with the people inside Belmullet in a different way from the people in Doohoma or Bangor. Sometimes this is associated with Irish. But I think most of the time it's associated with the Irish language only to the extent that colour is used as an identifying factor. But I believe these distinctions are deeper than that. To me it seems to reflect different populations, different colonisations. Castlebar is not this area.

CAITLÍN Shell of course didn't see or understand the people of this area. They came in here and thought there was nobody to stop them. 'You can go in there, they're grand people, there's no one there to do anything, just get the 'leaders' on your side and that's it.' They got an awful shock.

MICHEÁL It never occurred to them that they would have to

deal with the people of the area. Because they had all their dealing done. Their dealing was only necessary, as in any post-colonial country, on the level of those in charge. Who would you find in charge in Nigeria? It's not the old chiefs who hadn't the training for it – not the traditional leaders at all – it's the new civil service and the new politicians who were elected under this new imposed system. That's who they were used to dealing with wherever they were, whether in East Timor or Nigeria. They dealt with the post-colonial establishment as they would have seen it. Maybe they never analysed it like that. But that's how they would have seen how things work. Our establishment may be post-colonial but we are not.

CAITLÍN As we say in Irish, shíl siad nach raibh anseo ach scata amhais. They thought that there was nobody left in Erris, it's plagued by emigration, that the best people are gone. They never expected to have to meet people.

IRELAND FROM THE 1960s EMBRACED MULTINATIONAL DEVELOPMENT. WHY WAS THAT RESISTED HERE? ALL THE EVIDENCE WOULD HAVE SAID THIS WOULD BE WELCOMED, THAT PEOPLE WOULD BE DELIGHTED?

MICHEÁL I think that by the 1990s it had gone beyond that stage. The relationship between developers and their dependants, which obviously included the civil service, had gone beyond that stage. It had gone to the stage where it didn't occur to them at all that people counted, people anywhere. There was a Shell-sourced graphic in the Connaught Telegraph in August this year that shows Shell's ideal Erris – no houses, no people, no Broadhaven Bay and one little miserable dolphin as the only sign of life. Shell heaven – no people!

They didn't even have to consider attempting to con us about jobs. They were actually very reasonable about jobs from the word go. They were saying that there would be seventy permanent positions.

Now we know it would only be twenty-seven but that's only out by about three to one. They didn't put a huge amount of resources in at the start into pointing out to the people what the advantages would be. They said you'll all be rich, but only in a general sort of way. They didn't have to put the work in because the State system and its leadership had become so subservient to the multinationals that they had stopped caring, had stopped being careful.

What they are having to do now, that is actually consider what people are saying to them, is something they haven't had experience of for years and years. This is definitely so since the late 1980s when there was a final change from the old political guard to the next generation, the 'me generation'. The 'me generation' in public administration and in politics preceded the 'me generation' of ordinary people that has emerged in its present extent in the Celtic Tiger. We definitely have been led from the top by our leaders on this.

So, when the company came in here, they met with that political culture of dependency and facilitation.

For example, I know that when Enterprise Oil had their first formal meeting with the county councillors they expected to be stiffly questioned on the dangers of the project and on its risks and gains. Instead, what they got, and they were absolutely shocked and delighted about this, was 'jaysus, this is great, we have our own gas, God it will be great.' Every county councillor was simply seeing the gas as money for free! I can remember one councillor at the time issuing a statement saying that broadband was coming with the pipeline but it was only coming as far as Lahardane.

I had an image of a broadband pipe sticking up in the middle of the little square in Lahardane where people could go out and tap into it! That was actually the level of understanding. They didn't have to take seriously anything. All you had to do was go through the forms. I think the oil companies were very badly led astray on this as a result of this infatuation.

WHAT WERE YOUR FIRST DEALINGS WITH SHELL?

CAITLÍN We were here one night in 2000 and a neighbour came in to visit. Micheál had heard some inkling about it before that. There was the usual chat about things – bhfuil aon scéal agat? – and he said that he had heard that the gas was coming in and they are building something up in Ballinaboy. I said to him, bhuel, dá mbeadh aon mhaith ann ní thiocfadh sé anseo. That was my reaction. At the time I thought it would be done like Kinsale. So fine, I had no problem in the world with it.

MICHEÁL The first notification in the place really was an announcement in the Parish Newsletter that we were all going to be rich. That was in April 2000, I think. It was sometime afterwards that the then parish priest and the bishop were taken by helicopter dressed up in the benediction robes with a television crew out on to the rig. This was a source of huge scandal for people. People thought straight away what are they up to? This is a reversion to an abuse of power by the clergy. People of my age had seen this before. I remember a case of a priest who was leaving a particular house one day after a row and he cleaned his boots on the doorstep as he went out. Cursing the house. He is still alive. We were not that far away from that kind of mumbo-jumbo.

I had got word from a friend of mine who had been contacted by someone in the Department of Marine who said that there is an Environmental Impact Statement about to be prepared and unless the local fishermen put in some sort of a case there will be no consideration of the inshore fisheries in the EIS. I took a note of that on the 12th of April.

We heard then they had got a twenty-seven acre site up in Ballinaboy and that they were clearing it. Almost immediately they got two local JCBs in to do a bit of clearing and digging. Coillte had been doing a little bit of clear-felling on the site before that.

CAITLÍN The first thing we knew of it really was when they started calling around. Then we heard that there was to be a meeting in Belmullet. Micheál wasn't at it. They had also come to the pubs a couple of times.

MICHEÁL They started that in June 2000. They had a model of the terminal and they started carrying it around to the pubs and to the Coláiste. That was in September actually.

CAITLÍN They had a couple of meetings with the Rossport people.

MICHEÁL They held some meetings in pubs and started buying pints for people. Then they had 'information meetings'. But, they were very much out of place. They were highly dressed, smartly dressed, Louis Copeland-type people. They stuck out like a sore thumb.

They were telling the people how lucky they were, that it was as if the saviour had returned. I didn't go to any of the meetings because I don't go to those type of meetings, for indoctrination.

CAITLÍN There was a programme done then for Leárgas about it with the parish priest. Then they started sponsoring things like the golf club who got a bit of money for a classic. All the focus was on the terminal. There was no word of the pipeline at that stage.

MICHEÁL They were pretending at the early stage that the pipeline was to go on the far side of the estuary, at Pollathomas. It was to go above the graveyard there and then on to Ballinaboy. It became clearer later what they really intended but not then. I remember that year I said to the kids at school that I had no interest in it at all.

I was doing geography with them. I said to them that either this crowd don't know what they're doing or they know more than I know. It seemed that they were intending to sink this huge pipeline up the side of the hill which everyone knows will draw all the water into the drain and will take the side of the mountain down. This was Glengad Hill that was later destroyed by bog-slides. But this is a huge company, this is a huge industry, this is a marvellously technologically advanced industry and maybe they know something I don't know, I said. But to me it was stupid. But that was the extent of my interest in it.

In those early stages there was confusion and a huge push for it coming from the Catholic Church. The Council for the West, which had been set up by the western bishops, immediately organised an organisation called One Voice for Erris. They held meetings in the parish priest's house. It was attended by those with vested interests only and a couple of people who were very worried. In general, the people were very suspicious of it from the word go.

CAITLÍN What worried me all the time was that there was nobody asking questions. There were no questions. 'We were going to be rich. The schools will be full of kids'. But there were no questions being asked about the project or the dangers or the chimneys. That worried me.

MICHEÁL I had no idea at all of the implications of a thing like this. I thought it was a Kinsale-type development and that you obviously pay a price for any heavy industry and that there would be some health implications. But I wasn't really concerned. It wasn't something I could do anything about. I did see as a geographer that what they were doing was wrong, utterly stupid, but maybe they knew more than I did.

HOW DID UNCERTAINTY MOVE INTO OPPOSITION?

MICHEÁL For me it was later on in the autumn. Things had happened that I didn't know about. In early October there was a little piece in the paper about a press conference with Bertie Ahern and Frank Fahey. Enterprise Oil, Statoil, Marathon and Bord Gais were announcing a deal to build a pipeline from Ballinaboy to Galway. That surprised me because they hadn't applied for planning permission or anything at that stage. Yet the deal with Bord Gais was up and running. That surprised me but then I don't have any illusions about how the political system works. They haven't made much effort in Mayo up until now to hide the involvement of politics in business so it was easier to see. But it was the next year, in 2001, that the Fianna Fáil and Fine Gael councillors were whipped into a party frenzy to support the project. But, as I have said, in the early stages it was the Church which did the running.

CAITLÍN A landowner from Rossport, Monica Muller, rang here a few times. She was very worried about the terminal. Micheál then got interested and I got worried.

MICHEÁL Gerard Muller asked us to go over to the house one night and we went over. Gerard was showing us some of the information. There was a suggestion at the time that Powers Rolls Royce would build a power station in Bellacorrick. I understand the world out there and it was obvious that this proposed 64KW power station for Bellacorrick was utterly ridiculous. No one does that in this day and age in an isolated area. Perhaps you'd do it in the middle of Galway city for local power. But it's completely at variance with the reality. I knew there was something very fishy going on.

So Gerard and Monica said to me 'please go in and look at the Environmental Impact Statement'. In order to satisfy them more than anything else I went to look for it. Now, you had one copy announced to be available in the council offices in Castlebar, and one in the Garda barracks in Ballina and one in the Garda barracks in Belmullet. The police were brought on stage very early as the guardians of the golden grail. I found this very off-putting. They didn't even have a copy in the barracks in Glenamoy. The copy is probably still moulding out in Ballina because obviously nobody ever had a look at it. In Belmullet they got the fright of their lives when we started invading the place later on. That was the only access to the EIS at that stage that we had.

There was a huge meeting called then organised by the Church and The Council for the West that same night. Leading it at this stage were leading figures in the Council for the West such as Sean Hannick and Dr Seamus Caulfield and the priests – the nuns are more aware normally. They had this big meeting called for the convent in Belmullet. All the priests in the area were supposed to be there. I had gone to Belmullet that day to have a look at the EIS with Bríd my daughter, and two neighbours, Treasa Ní Ghearraigh and Uinsionn MacGraith. It was then that I saw what was planned. There were two volumes in the EIS at that stage. We went and skimmed through things. There was one page I always remember where they gave the results of tests from a single well. They gave a list of the 'little uglies' that were included in the gas. I was horrified. I had a general look at it fast and saw what they intended to do. There was run-off from the terminal site proposed to go straight into Carrowmore Lake through perforated drains. You'd thought that 'perforated' made them something! And also Sruhwaddoccon on this side would get its share of it.

The guards handed it out to us in the hall, in the lobby of the barracks. After about half an hour a guard came out to us and said, 'oh God, you're still here, I never thought you'd still be here, come in.' He took us in to one of the interrogation rooms where we could sit down. We had a look then at some of the drawings they had. They had a drawing of where the outlet pipe from the terminal was to go where they intended to dump the water with all the uglies in. It was just a few kilometres from landfall – not from land, for of course the bay is a long, narrow bay. There was of course no understanding at all that the bay has a tow inwards instead of out. These were spatial realities that struck me immediately. The chemical mix was horrifying. Treasa, Uinsionn and myself came home but Bríd stayed on in Belmullet and went into this huge meeting. There had been a number of these intimidatory-type meetings although I don't know why they were trying to be intimidatory then. There was no real opposition to it yet at all. Planning permission had just been applied for. Anyway, Bríd came home and she couldn't get over the stupidity of it. No one obviously knew what they were talking about. The unreality was so pervasive at that stage that one leading figure boasted that, 'I am one of those who wine and dine on a regular basis with Enterprise Oil.' I could find my ears getting red with náire (shame) when I heard this. It was a matter of a boast that only the elite had an opportunity to wine and dine with the developers of this wonderful project. Coming from a bright man with experience of the world that showed the extent of the suspension of disbelief. They were codding themselves.

CAITLÍN That comment was made in response to Sr. Majella McCarron. Sr. Majella had seen in the paper that there was going to be this meeting in Belmullet. She thought that she better go down and help the local priest because it was an oil company trying to come in to his parish. She had been working in Nigeria for many years and knew Ken Sara Wiwa. So she came down and the parish priest met her at the train and brought her in. It was only then she realised that these people wanted Enterprise Energy in! She spoke at the meeting and she said to them that those people will try everything to get in. She told him of her experience in Nigeria. She said that they'll wine and dine you. And that was the response from one of them!

MICHEÁL And in public! Majella found that instead of the Church supporting the people as she had expected, as they had done in Nigeria, here you had the very opposite! The Church had been co-opted into the thing as advocates. She got a different lift back!

We got copies of the EIS then and went through it. I didn't know what to do because we had never objected to anything in our lives. I didn't know anything about the planning system, nothing at all, we were red raw. We didn't yet know about the Statutory Instruments that had been introduced by Bertie Ahern.

Meanwhile, there was the launch of a project that had been funded by Mayo County Council and An Taisce on sustainable tourism in the coastal regions. I had given some slight help to the researcher who had put the report together. It was being launched in early December in Castlebar. We were invited to the launch so I went up. Normally I wouldn't go to things like that. I said to the researcher do you realise what is being put in the middle of your report area? She said what is it? I told her and asked her if you had known that would your report have been different? She said indeed it would. I said can you give me an opportunity of talking tonight in the lion's den so to speak. So she called on me at one point and I took the opportunity to say to the councillors and officials and journalists there that this was a huge project and that it needed to be looked at very, very seriously. They were not aware that there was an issue around this at all. One thing that was very interesting on that night was that a person from the planner's office whom I didn't know said to me would you please put in an objection of some sort. Now this was early December 2000. She said we in the planning section have no idea that there is any issue about this. We had no idea that this had to be considered or taken seriously. If you put in an objection fast, she said, at least we'll be forced to look at it. That was the extent of awareness within the planning section of Mayo County Council.

That same day Padraig Hughes had resigned as County Secretary and the great and good had been partying. Hughes let it be known that he didn't expect anything for Mayo from the project. He is now on Shell's payroll.

CAITLÍN Meanwhile there were the meetings taking place in Rossport.

MICHEÁL I wasn't involved in those. However, what was happening was being related to me and I was enjoying the accounts! They were talking about the pipeline and the pipeline was going left and right and everywhere!

CAITLÍN We did not go to any of the meetings because we

would not want to interfere with anything the Rossport people wanted to do with their land.

MICHEÁL Land was a different issue. There was no doubt that for me the real issue was health. My main concern was the emissions from the terminal. The pipeline for me wasn't an issue at that stage. By then I had become aware of what was coming in but the full implications hadn't actually struck me. I had to try and take on board then all the different aspects of the project. The pipeline was very much on the long finger. They applied for planning permission for the terminal and this made the terminal the focus.

Looking at it even now, my concerns really started with that page in the EIS. There were all of these nasties plus nitrogen oxide plus sulphurs of various sorts with implications for people's health. Suddenly we discovered a huge amount of stuff. For example, we discovered that you couldn't object to the terminal on the basis of health because that only came for consideration when the terminal was up and the EPA were asked for a licence. I didn't even have any suspicion of the lack of seriousness of the EPA at that stage, their lack of independence, their lack of a feel for their authority and responsibility. The mercury was one thing that got me at the start. There were no scrubbers in the chimneys to scrub the mercury out. I knew the implications of mercury for expectant mothers and unborn babies. I was very aware of that. This was to be burned off into the air where much of it would come down on the local population. For me there was no issue at that stage but the health. So, I started studying it with the help of the Internet and what information I had. Suddenly, the enormity of what they were doing to the population struck me. For the Rossport people at that stage it was the pipeline that they were most worried about. Others like Brid McGarry were very concerned from the start about the health effects from the terminal. The Ballinaboy and Léana Mór residents, the nearest to the terminal, strongly opposed the terminal. I couldn't see that we had any hope of winning anything or stopping anything. The matter of stopping it never entered my mind. All that entered my mind at that stage was that we were dealing with the most powerful entities in the world and they were obviously doing a cobbled job.

WHERE DID YOUR CONFIDENCE COME FROM TO OPPOSE THE PROJECT? WHY DID YOU NOT ACCEPT THE ASSURANCES OF THE VARIOUS EXPERTS AND REGULATORY BODIES?

CAITLÍN Because we didn't trust them – even less now.

MICHEÁL For me, a very important part of that process was when an English company had been hired by Enterprise Oil to do a report on the circulation of wastewater when it was dumped out in the bay, using a standard model for this called Proteus. The company had made it clear in the report that they had not got enough information to do it. They made it clear that all the information they were using had been supplied by Enterprise Oil. It was obvious for example that the company didn't know that there was a tow in instead of a tow out. It was obvious that they didn't like what they were doing.

They were paid for it and I made it clear in the submission that I made that I respected the approach of the company because they were obviously professionals who were aware of their reputations. And at the same time the County Council and everybody else were prepared to push ahead.

There was obviously no trust in the council. Then, Enterprise had to withdraw their first planning application. They put in the second application in April 2001 and they used some of the work that this consultant company had done but did not use other aspects of it.

CAITLÍN I had no reason to have any meas (respect) on the council. They usually treat people in this area with disdain, with no respect. This goes back a long way. I remember a time when people were afraid to have three hens in their garden or they'd lose the dole! If there was a dog barking around the place the inspector would believe there were animals being kept. There was a history of dreading officials who came in from outside.

MICHEÁL The submission we had made to the council was picked up and given front page in The Western People, ironically under the by-line of Christy Loftus, who has now, in his own written words, 'taken the shilling.' It got a huge heading using 'waffle' and 'contempt' quoted from our submission! It was in one of these silly seasons that newspapers have after Christmas when people have nothing else to do. That was the first objection that became a matter of public record. It attracted a lot of attention at the time. I said that some of the things that Enterprise Oil were proposing were straight out of the teddy bear's picnic such as spreading peat a metre or two metres high among the trees. It was science fiction stuff.

**THERE WERE NO FACE TO FACE TALKS
WITH ENTERPRISE AT ANY POINT.**

CAITLÍN They never wanted to meet those who weren't in favour.

MICHEÁL Around that time we circulated every TD and all the councillors in Mayo with our concerns. We did a huge job.

There was a meeting in Glenamoy between the first submission by Enterprise and the second one in April 2001. That was the last effort by the bishop and The Council for the West to present The One Voice for Erris as a realistic body. That was the last time the bishop came out in public. He left it to his acolytes after that.

CAITLÍN That meeting in Glenamoy was well rigged up beforehand. Micheál wasn't going to go at all and a few here asked him to please come to the meeting. So he went.

MICHEÁL I have seen the way the politicians always work ever since I've come here. They work in a very simple way by working people up and getting them so excited that they have to go to the pub immediately afterwards and drink. Next morning they've a hangover and that's the end of it. The politicians meanwhile have gone away laughing at us. I've seen again and again the way they sideline people by working them up. What the people have forgotten is that democracy can only function when you hold the elected representatives to account. It cannot work otherwise.

There were a number of interesting things about the meeting in Glenamoy. A local councillor was there who also happens to be a Statoil agent. He went on that night about all that he was doing for the Ballinaboy people and how marvellous it was. One of them said, 'but we didn't ask you.' Even at that stage was absolutely no trust in the politicians at all. Then, a pe asked him whether he had read the EIS? 'Oh I've read the important bits,' he replied. That became a great saying around here – don't worry about it, he has read the important bits! Indeed, another supporter of the project replied to the same question in a television interview that the EIS wasn't written for the likes of him! He's a second-level school principal – he was probably right!

But at that meeting in Glenamoy, the bishop and the parish priest were on the stage as One Voice for Erris. There was also a representative from the Irish Offshore Operators Association there. He was the advisor on natural resources for the Council for the West based in Donegal and a supplier to Enterprise Oil. As the night went on there was stronger and stronger support for us. The supporters of the project who had gone up thinking that this was going to be another fascist victory disappeared into the background. As the meeting went on, and more fishermen and farmers were coming in, the more it became obvious that it wasn't wanted. The hall was packed. The bishop saw eventually that things were going wrong, that they weren't going in the way he had expected. He said 'now, we'll appoint a committee tonight that will represent the concerns of the people here and that will prepare questions to ask of Enterprise Oil'. That was the extent of what the bishops and the establishment were going to demand of Enterprise Oil – that they would answer questions! It was so lacking in any real context. So I stood up immediately and I said that, without prejudice to any decision this meeting might come to, people like me and the Ballinaboy people and the Leenamore people would carry on doing exactly what they had been doing until now, that is fighting their own battle against the project but keeping communication with each other. That was the first time this new approach – new for an area like this – to campaigning was made public. The bishop almost immediately stood up and walked out.

CAITLÍN There was no committee set up.

MICHEÁL The opposition has remained consistent all the time. You had a small number of people with a vested interest who thought they would make immediate money on it. A small number of them obviously favoured the project from the start. You had a small number of people like us who would be directly affected by the project and who had read up about it, knew what the dangers were and who were opposed to it. And then you had the mass of the people of Erris who were very worried about it, who didn't like the idea but who wouldn't make a fuss about opposing it. The vast majority were concerned.

That became very clear when TG4 had their programme Árdán in Belmullet at that time. There was a debate about it on stage in front of an audience. But obviously the programme was prepared on the understanding that this would be the blow to the opposition that would sweep the ground from under them. Then the presenter called for a show of hands from those who supported it. Six voted for it! Everyone else in the place voted against it. The presenter was obviously shocked. The promoters were never prepared to admit that the vast majority of the people don't want this or they have strong worries about it.

The various decision-making bodies didn't pay real attention to the issue either. I only dealt with the County Council in writing. But many of the other people involved called into their offices in Castlebar. At various times, they were refused photocopies. Other times they'd get them but be held up all day. There was all this petty bureaucracy nonsense trying to frighten people, trying to intimidate them.

For the Department of the Marine there was this project to be advanced and that was their objective only. They paid us no attention. There was obviously a huge lack of knowledge in the Department. They weren't ready for a huge project like this at all. For example they expected to push the pipeline through as part of the foreshore licence. When they found out they couldn't they simply changed the law as Michael Daly of the Petroleum Affairs Division told us they would.

When I saw how the Health and Safety Authority were dealing with the health issues and that the EPA didn't want to become involved at all, it suddenly occurred to me that these were the people, with the County Council, that were responsible for the health and safety of heavily populated areas like Castlebar and Westport and Ballina. Whatever chance we in an isolated rural area would have of getting away with mistakes in infrastructure, you'd have no chance in a town. So if this is the standard that they are applying in Castlebar, Ballina, Westport, Claremorris, then there is some awful disaster facing us down the road. The more we were dealing with them the more we realised that the concern of these bodies was their own survival and appeasing the powerful and not the agenda they were given by the electorate.

The agenda given by the people, to serve the people, that came very much down the line. Instead, the first job they did was to look after themselves, to look after their own system.

THAT MUST HAVE LED YOU TO DESPAIR ABOUT CONTEMPORARY IRELAND?

MICHEÁL It did. It did until last summer after we went into jail. I could say honestly that I regretted having wasted my time contributing all my life to this awful system, to this denial, to this con democracy, this cod democracy, that was being administered by cod civil servants, cod public servants. Because that is all I could call them. I mean contributing both as a teacher and even in just living here. In a way I had wasted forty years functioning in an environment that I found out didn't exist.

I remember quite early on, when we had objected the first time, the Connaught Telegraph newspaper ran an anonymous column under the by-line 'Tallyman' blaming 'outsiders' for delaying the project. So Monica Muller and I reported them under the Incitement to Hatred legislation. They backed off a bit then.

CAITLÍN That was why on the day of the rally last year in Castlebar I gave a rundown of how he got involved in Rossport and how he came to the area. They hadn't used his name but we knew well they were talking about Micheál and Monica.

I feel let down by the system, let down by our politicians, let down by our county councillors. We were reared as children to obey the law and we did the same with our own children. And all of a sudden you feel you're out on your own, you've elected those people to look after us, and all of a sudden they're not looking after us.

MICHEÁL When I came to this area I stayed here and apart

from some Conradh na Gaelige work and development work with an I.R.D. pilot scheme, Leader and Meitheal Mhaigh Eo, I had involved myself locally.

I was born in 1940. When Clann na Poblachta was founded in 1947 my father became involved with them. Many of the kind of people I had grown up with at home, the kind of people I knew, the politicians who had come to the house, had been involved in the War of Independence. These were people like Donnacha O Bríain, one of the first generation Fianna Fáil people; Tadgh Crowley a local Fianna Fáil TD, a gentle quiet man; Jimmy Collins, who I knew from my cousins and who was a small man's man; Stevie Coughlin, who was a bottom-line man; Ted Russell who ended up in Fine Gael but was a Clann man, a public school, well-educated man, a businessman in Limerick; McBride and Hartnett.

Frank Ryan came from the next parish and Knocklong, the other half-parish, had a soviet in Cleeves' factory in 1920. This was the kind of political environment I grew up in, quite varied, an environment of argument and discussion about things. We knew there was mickey mouse stuff going on in the background – who'd get the job of rate collector and this kind of stuff – but it wasn't basic.

The personalities I had known in politics were the personalities who had come out of the War of Independence and the Civil War and those who reacted to it. They were people who had put their lives on the line and who believed in what they were doing. Ted Russell died early on this year. He was 92 or 93, one of the last of the Clann na Poblachta TDs. To find out how we had degenerated, how the manning of the political system had deteriorated, was a shock to me.

The public bodies didn't see it as their function to make decisions on their merits. Because of that it was not possible for them to listen. Their function was to do what they were told. The top authority had made a decision that this project was going through and that was that. There was to be no discussion. There was no sense of reality at all. They were not able – they were not allowed – to engage with the project at all. For example, the County Council admitted that they didn't have the expertise in-house to assess the project but they said that they would hire expertise and that it would all be done properly. They never did.

IT TOOK CONFIDENCE TO TAKE ON THE SYSTEM, SO WHERE DID THE RESOURCES TO DO THAT COME FROM?

MICHEÁL I suppose there is a feeling of solidarity that we are all in the same boat. For me, the kind of person I am, I tried to stretch myself as far as possible, to fill obvious gaps in our knowledge. I had to do this in order to send in submissions and so on. For example, we had no one to deal with the peat so I said, OK I'll handle that. Bríd McGarry was dealing with the emissions because she had a qualification in food science. The Ballinaboy people had contact with English consultants on emissions. Gerard Muller did a frightening study of the bridges in Erris. So we were looking coldly at what technical resources we had. We were working individually though we were helping each other. But we were very much aware – at least I was very much aware – that we were probably dealing with the best in the world. I didn't think we had a chance at all.

CAITLÍN Many people wouldn't have the ability to study it like that. I'd feel like sitting here giving out about whatever they were doing but I might not be able to put it down on paper. I certainly wouldn't stand up in front of a crowd and say what I wanted to say. I made the tea during the last six years and he sat and worked! That man worked from morning until night on all sorts of documents and research work. I kind of sat back and ran the house if you like and the garden while he studied it. He had the ability to do that. I certainly wouldn't. I'd get very angry about things.

MICHEÁL The kind of networks that we belonged to – locally and through Conradh na Gaeilige, traditional music, the development work I had done – all helped in getting support. These are informal networks that touch the real people who are exposed to the effects of bad planning in their daily lives.

If any one of us had a victory then more people would come and have a look. We were making sure that the information was getting out. I would always try – I suppose it's an old-fashioned teacher thing – to get as much information out as possible. And according as people were finding out more about it, it was obvious to them that this is wrong. And according as we were picking up technical information we were trying to spread it,

trying to get it out there. Our aim was not to get it into the
national media. It was to get it into the unofficial network that
is there, where real people live, but not the sheltered
establishment.

CAITLÍN The other thing about any campaign is that if you
believe that you are right and you are telling the truth and then
are able to stand up and speak what you believe to be the truth
and defend it, then that will give you the confidence to do the
other things. That's what I believe. For example, if Micheál said
something at a meeting or at the oral hearing for instance and
they would immediately contradict him he could use language
and come back at them. He'd know he was right. He'd have his
facts and figures. That was a great help. Whereas I'd read
something and forget in ten minutes what I'd read. Again, it's
that ability thing. But when you know that what's happening is
wrong and that you're on the right side, that does your
confidence good. That's what kept me fired up when they went
to jail.

MICHEÁL Our attachment to place comes into it too.
According as we were going on bit by bit and learning more it
was obvious that it was the end of the place as somewhere to
which the next generation could return whether visiting or
otherwise. This was the end of it. It wasn't just a matter of new
industry coming in – that alone is no problem – but that it would
be the end of millennia of culture. For us, the cultural aspect
was very simple. When people talk about culture it's a page in
the Times that no one reads or the Sunday newspaper. But for
us it's a different thing, it's all of living, everyday survival.

CAITLÍN It's your being.

MICHEÁL It involves the people you know and the place.
I remember last May my family were home during the holidays.
I remember on a weekend the four of them were down here
visiting and were worried I suppose. I said to them 'it's likely I'll
be in jail next time I see you.' And they said 'yeah, we know
that.' It was a casual acceptance that this is wrong and you will
go the whole way. There wasn't any opposition in the family.
There seems to have been an acceptance of this. It was very

simple. This is wrong. It sounds very childish and a very easy thing to say.

CAITLÍN It takes over your life too. There were two rooms taken up with all the books and papers and forms. There were days when we hardly spoke a word until sleeping time. I'd be doing this and he'd be at that!

We were reared to obey the law and to have respect for authority – the police, civil servants, you name it. And we reared our own kids in the same way. And at the end of the day I don't know whether I did the right thing or not to be quite honest. You obey the law and have respect for our government and then they turn around and try to do this to our area and to our people. We elected them to look after us. They're not doing it. How do they rear their children?

I think the conclusion is that it is a banana republic at the end of the day. You saw that especially when the men were sent into prison. You don't know the sinking feeling I've had for the last six years about this country that had been fought and died for. It would leave you now lifeless almost. I loved history when I was going to school and I was nearly out there fighting the battles. And then to see what has happened! We were told for as long as I remember that there's nothing in Erris, there's nothing in Mayo. But now there's billions of euros worth of oil and gas just a couple of miles there off our shores here. And we're not going to benefit one bit except for a couple of jobs. They would take it and walk on us and take it through Erris and through Mayo without gain for the country or Erris or Mayo except that they will destroy this area. And whoever would live to see the day in thirty or forty years time there will be nobody living along Sruhwaddoccon and that area. If this happens and the big pipe goes in and the terminal in Ballinaboy, people will not be there. Number one, they won't get planning permission anyway for their house and two, they wouldn't want to live there. As a parent I wouldn't want to see my children building a house along Sruhwaddoccon or Glengad.

This is not the country I thought it was. It's an awful shock and shattering experience. Life is gone from us.

MICHEÁL I was the youngest of nine who survived. A brother died of appendicitis in 1942. My father and mother got married on the day the Civil War broke out. My mother in particular would have been strongly of the republican side. My father would have been generally that way but he wouldn't have done anything about it. He hunted and fished and played football and hurling and that kind of thing. My mother wasn't actively involved but she was very strongly connected. There were four in my mother's family – the Miss Hurleys they were called. An aunt of mine was in Cumann na mBan. She wrote poetry. She loved Irish songs though she hadn't a word of Irish. There was a very strong emotional commitment to the concept of Ireland, to a country where it would be a good place to live and where there would be improvements for people. As I said before, my father even joined Clann na Poblachta when it came.

With me I would always have had a strongly republican way of looking at things, as opposed to a feudal, royalist, oligarchical rule. I would have seen the border as being a disaster. The very fact of it being there has made it a constant cause of conflict. But I never became involved in any way until I knew the guns were over in 1994. Then there was the possibility of undoing the damage that de Valera did in 1927 by forming a partitionist party where he could have done the opposite. For me there is an underlying political aspect. I got involved in issues like the Irish language because it was State policy, the policy of the Irish people, to revive Irish. I was reared in an area where there was no Irish. I came to this area, Rossport and Ceathrú Thaidhg, effectively because of a commitment to national policy. If I had been in Finland I would probably have done the same. I would have been a supporter of the Finns against the Swedish cultural domination of the time. But suddenly I find out that the entire basis on which my life was being lived was a con. It's an awful situation. The entire basis!

CAITLÍN I cried that evening they were sent to prison with anger and frustration. I was so proud of him. And afterwards I shed tears for my father. And I could cry today again.

MICHEÁL I came into this area out of a commitment. In my last year in university I was president of the students' union and head of the Cumunn Éigse, the first to combine the two. I acted in the Taidbhearc. I did debating and attended the Lit and Deb every week. I was an obvious character for politics in those days. But I came here because they needed a teacher. This was my entire life's commitment. I suppose it was nearly a communist-type thing or a missionary thing!

It's been a huge blow. In my last year in university I remember attending a conference being held in Galway. I welcomed the delegates to Galway and made a grand speech. Gerry Collins came up to me afterwards. He went on to become a government minister and was involved in student politics at the time. He said to me, 'that was a great speech you gave Micheál, but I'd ease off on the Irish. A bit of Irish is grand.' Just a bit – don't overdo it! People might think you believe in 'national identity'. That wouldn't do at all!

But for me there wasn't any question. They couldn't find teachers for Rossport. There was a new school but with no stability. They were in great difficulties so I said fine, I'll go over and do it. I know that it would have been looked down upon, looked at objectively from outside. I know that it would have been said that he was an awful amadán, that he had put his entire career backwards or ended his career. It would have been looked at as a total waste of time. But for me it was very simple. We accepted State policy for ourselves and then for our children.

DID THE EVENTS OF LAST SUMMER NOT SHOW THAT THERE WERE STILL IDEALS AMONG MANY PEOPLE?

CAITLÍN Yes, it's there if it could get out. With all this greed we have I think it's very difficult for it to. I would blame the Catholic Church for a lot of it in the 1970s when the whole curriculum was changed in the teaching of Christian doctrine in the national schools. We had to change a lot of it then because it was high time it changed from the question-and-answer format. I had to teach it through English to Irish-speaking children. I am very sorry I didn't stand up and tell the bishop that I refused. That was the policy of the diocese. I was a young teacher at the time. The majority of the children had no English and they learned all those difficult questions through English for their first holy communion and so on. Ach sin scéal eile! They were putting all the emphasis on 'me, me, me', and 'my, my, my', and 'I'm the greatest thing since the flood'. I know it's important to instil confidence in young people but it was all an emphasis on 'me'. I think it started there with the Church as well as with our governments and our people as a whole. It was all me and me and I said at meetings what about us, us, us, we're living within families and communities. Oh that will come later, they said. But it's what you do at those early ages between four and seven that is going to stick. I came home a couple of times from those meetings with the diocesan examiner and other teachers to examine different options about how it was to be taught and I cried. This was thirty years ago. That culture is still out there. Hopefully it might change.

MICHEÁL For me I could see the change in the quality of the political people. I could compare the political people who were around my house when I was a child. I've mentioned some of them earlier. Look what we have got in their place – Ray Burke, Frank Fahey! I said – and our children used to be annoyed with me – I said in recent years that I've wasted my life. I wasted forty years. It was very obvious to me that I had spent forty years on a chimera. But not now. I can see hope now again. Opposing Shell's project here was just a continuation of what I had always stood for. It was wrong and I would have had great difficulties facing myself if I hadn't opposed it.

EVEN TO THE POSSIBILITY OF IMPRISONMENT?

MICHEÁL It was a process. I knew from as soon as Shell got planning permission from An Bord Pleanála and as soon as they moved onto the pipeline that, bit by bit, prison was the next step. I could not avoid it. And I couldn't see beyond that because I couldn't see how we would get out of jail. Because in the last few years we have learned a huge amount about systems and how they work and I knew that if convicted on a contempt of court you would have to apologise and I knew I could not apologise for something that was not wrong. So I saw that imprisonment would be quite long. I accepted that because we didn't have any choice. From the time we went in to prison I said from the word go that it would be October anyway because the full court hearing was set for October. I believed it would be like that because I had no faith at that stage in any system of the Irish State. I believed they would get a permanent injunction and that that would be no good to us at all. I didn't see any quick way out at all. I thought this is the way it goes.

At that stage I did not believe that the people would really care. I believed that the people were too busy in the consumer society we're in. They were too busy trying to survive. Many of the people who were at the age to be activists had mortgages that were killing them. Their money and wages were going on loans. People nowadays have got fine incomes but their incomes are nearly all gone on loans, gone before they get them! They have to live to a high standard of living. So I believed they were too busy to care. They had so much on their plate that they couldn't.

At the time of our imprisonment there was a sense of inevitability about the project. Everything was going ahead. I couldn't see any prospects of success. Willie all the time said it's not coming in, but to me that made no sense at all. To me the game was up. But we still had no choice because it was wrong. Winning didn't come into it at all at that stage. It was just something one had to do.

CAITLÍN I was prepared for it as well. I thought it would be a long haul in prison. The response of the people before they went in was that this is inevitable, it's going to be brought in. I'm told that a local councillor Frank Chambers still says 'it's coming in whether you like it or not.' I had that feeling myself for a good few years. I was losing faith in the government. I saw that whatever the authorities wanted to do they would do regardless of whether it's the right thing. An awful lot of the people thought that. For me I thought that – win or lose – we will fight this to the bitter end. It was wrong, wrong, wrong and we had to stand up.

But in going to prison I knew nothing about law or courts or anything. I thought that they'd probably get a month. But what happened was they were put in and they were going to be left in until they purged their contempt. But I couldn't see that coming easily from them.

I was very angry the day they were sent to prison. I knew they would be imprisoned. I was very angry. The children were there. They were all in tears and very upset, especially when the judge said to Micheál, have you a house, have you a car, well then you should think of your wife and children. And as soon as they heard that – because he would always have looked after his

family in every way possible – they all burst into tears. I didn't.
I got mad. Our son Padraig was so upset. They all were. They
were all around their dad before he was taken away. But I was
very angry.

I had believed in the justice system. Not that I knew anything
about it. We were led to believe that justice would be done.
When I heard that judge and the way that he spoke to the
Rossport Five I will never ever forget it. He spoke in such a
contemptuous manner to them as if they were only... you'd have
more respect for a beetle falling on the floor than he had for
those men there.

There were people there from Shell in the court. I was sitting
behind them. I kept my eyes closely on them and they did not
expect the men to go to jail. When the judge had sent them off
to consider what was before them I think at that stage even
Shell were hoping that the men would back down.

When the men were sentenced all hell broke lose. We went
over as far as the Bridewell. People were crying and roaring. I
couldn't cry, I was so mad. I was just angry. That evening
Padraig and I went up to Mountjoy to bring up his medication.
And they were just leaving Mountjoy when we went up to the
gate. They were in the van. There were about thirty people there.
Sr. Majella McCarron was there and some Sinn Féin people and
Socialist Workers Party were there, people who had nothing to
do with it but for the anger they had. And then Padraig drove me
out to Cloverhill. And there were about ten or twelve people
outside Cloverhill.

MICHEÁL The people from those political parties provided the
same thing that ex-British army soldiers from the First World
War provided in the War of Independence – they provided the
organisational skills. I was intrigued at the way it worked out. I
still am. The political party activists from the Socialist Party, the
Socialist Workers Party, the Greens, Sinn Féin, independents
and from the bigger parties, became involved at an
organisational skills level. They did not become involved at a
party political level and still don't.

I wasn't surprised at being sent to jail because it was just
inevitable. We had broken the injunction and the inevitable
thing was to go to jail. There are questions about whether the
injunction should have been granted in the first place. Judge

Finnegan should not have because, as he said in court, he didn't know whether he should have given it or not. If you have doubt the status quo should remain, or so I thought. But we were sent to prison because we had defied his decision.

I had no idea what I was facing at all in prison. I didn't know anything about jail. It turned out to be much better than I would have expected if I had analysed it. As far as I was concerned I would just do what I was told and that was that. As far as I was concerned, going into jail was the end of the campaign. I thought that Shell would now go ahead with the project outside and finish it off. I couldn't see any other outcome the entire time. To me it was the end of it but I didn't have any choice. I didn't go into jail hoping that that would somehow change things outside. From now on people might be doing that. Going to jail as an option might become part of campaigns from now on. But I was just going to jail. It was the end of it, the end of the campaign. There would be a fuss for a couple of days, I thought, there would be a bit in the papers and then it would be forgotten about. Because to me the people in the area had been defeated at that stage. And they were defeated at that stage.

HOW DID YOU COPE IN PRISON?

MICHEÁL I didn't find the prison experience frightening. It just had to be gone through.

CAITLÍN I didn't have too many worries for him in prison. He had loved boarding school! Now, I hated boarding school. Every single hour I spent in boarding school was torture. But he liked it. I said to myself that any man who loved boarding school will be able for prison! However I was worried about his health. He had had heart problems in the previous few years.

MICHEÁL Time passed quickly enough in prison. The difficult times of the day if you didn't have visitors were from ten to twelve and from two to four. They were the difficult times. Apart from that I had no difficulty. I got books ready once I had enough stuff in for reading. I had no problem with keeping the place tidy, the housekeeping, etc. Once I got in, I developed a food routine. You were plied with food there. Obviously they've removed food out of the category of complaints in prison. The food was absolutely unbelievable. I had to make a decision on that to cut out the afternoon tea entirely or else put on weight. We decided as well to use prison clothes. It was as handy. You'd go down on Monday morning or Tuesday and leave your uniform into the laundry and you'd get a new set back.

An assistant warden told us the first night that the five of us should keep to ourselves. He advised us not mix, that this was no picnic in here. The morning after, as soon as we'd gone through the ten to twelve o'clock walk in the yard, we knew that this wouldn't work. By the end of the first day we knew that it was obvious that the prisoners didn't want this sticking to ourselves. Immediately then we went out to the lads and talked to them. From ten to twelve and from two to four you had to go out to the yard and walk around. We were together two or three of us most of the time anyhow. The prisoners had to make a distinction from then on, not us. We had no difficulty with them at all. They were fantastic. One of the lads – I don't know how long he was in for – he was waiting for trial, he came to me early on and he said to me, 'I'm telling you this, I guarantee you that there's no one going to hassle you here. They know what they'll get if they do. No one will hassle you. You'll be perfectly safe.' I had no worries after that.

There was tea at four o'clock. You were locked into the cell and you were in until twenty past five. You were left out again from twenty past five until seven. But you were allowed stay in at that time if you wanted. I normally stayed in unless I had a phone call. You had one phone call in the day. Sometimes you wouldn't be able to make the call in the morning or in the afternoon. I had tablets to collect at that time as well. There was also milk that you could get too. Then you were locked in from ten past seven until ten past eight the following morning. That was a very long spell.

We had TV in the room. No radio though. You could get a radio brought in but it could take six weeks to get it through the checking system. They had to send it out to some special place where it was opened and taken apart to ensure there was nothing dangerous in it. So in that way we were in tune with most of the big news anyway and the news about ourselves. I didn't watch it much but it was useful when the London bombings happened and the floods in New Orleans. There were fourteen or fifteen different stations. TV was more important in the life of some of the other prisoners than for us. If anything occurred, if some of our people would be on the early morning, I wouldn't know that they were going to be on, someone would always tell us, 'your daughter was on this morning' or 'your wife was on this morning'. The other prisoners would keep us in touch. Indeed the warders would as well. We were obviously a nuisance to the warders because there was an extra problem of care for them in looking after us. However, we were perfectly safe unless someone flipped entirely but that could happen anywhere. We were safe but the warders couldn't take that for granted.

After the first rally in Castlebar we were being told that things were changing outside, that it was different out there. 'Everyone is for you', and we'd say yeah sure, it's great. But then we started to get details. Bit by bit we realised that it was a different environment out there. I remember I got a letter in Irish from a woman in Spiddal with a cheque in it to go into the account, which I couldn't do until I came out. It was 150 euros or something like that. But that woke me up. Here was a woman in Connemara who didn't know me – she had heard me singing at some time, that was all – and here she was obviously angry.

Then the postcards and letters came. I got two letters from two kids in a secondary school in Dublin. This was later on. They were just back to school in September. They were in transition year. The whole class had discussed the Rossport Five immediately they came back in school. I knew then that this is different. At that stage we were getting up to 150 cards, from the Galway area in particular. We got a card from all the nuns in a Dublin convent signed by them all individually. Then we found out that there were people out campaigning in Galway. There was a man out full-time with a stall in Shop Street in Galway collecting signatures and giving out information. We'd say to ourselves inside what did we do for this, what did we do for these people? We did nothing for them: they didn't agree!

I would say the lack of understanding by the politicians outside helped us. They immediately came in to us and saw it as an opportunity for themselves. After a while other politicians, Green party people, Labour and Independents came in, who had a great understanding of the situation. We found that we could talk easily to them knowing we'd be safe. Obviously the politicians were embarrassed in Mayo but at the same time they saw it as an opportunity to get publicity. They'd prefer if we weren't in jail but given that we were there was an opportunity for them to get kudos in it. They totally misunderstood the situation. Enda Kenny came in to us to say, 'we'll get you out.' He immediately came out from jail and he made use of the fact for his own benefit. They misunderstood the situation so much that they believed that to get a bit of credibility they had to get us out of jail. We had to explain to them again and again, to Kenny and people like that who didn't want to listen, that the central issue was not to get us out of jail. We could walk out of jail any day we liked by purging our contempt. The issue was not getting us out of jail. We were not in jail in order to get out of jail. We were in jail because of the safety issue outside. So their lack of understanding of the situation actually helped us I think in a strange way. It was obvious that they weren't able to commit to the issues we were raising or even care. Their Rosary was 'the Terms can't be changed'.

We were hearing from Waterford, we were hearing from Cork, Kerry, Galway Sligo, Belfast – all over the country. We got cards from Omagh. We were getting contact from all over the country, ordinary, normal people saying 'you're doing great, you're doing it for us.' That's what changed it I would say for me. Here we had at least a hundred people a day saying to us that you're doing it for us, thank you for doing it for us. This is what changed it for me and made it into the kind of country I would be proud of. It was then that I started saying that it's great to be able to say I'm proud of being Irish again. Because all these people were saying that you're doing it for us. This of course suited the kind of way I looked at the world anyhow. This was the amazing thing. This belief that people had! 'Example for our kids!'

The prisoners too had changed. They admired us at the start. They thought we were great, we were giving McDowell a poke in the eye! But then, they would say, 'all you have to say is you're sorry and they'd let you out? Jaysus, I wouldn't be here for long!' But it changed. After a month they were saying 'don't give in to them.' I remember one American businessman came in to see me in jail and when he was leaving he turned around and put up his fist and said 'don't give in to them.' He later visited Bertie Ahern! The very same reaction as the prisoners had. It was 'them' and 'they'. People were identifying with us.

I found that liberating, not a burden. It helped us a lot that we were able to say at that stage to the warders and so on that we can't go out now, sure no one would talk to us if we go out! We can't go anywhere. We'd be lynched if we go to Waterford or Galway. They'd dump us in the Corrib! It wasn't a pressure because at the same time we were going nowhere anyway and it was strengthening us. Where we were we were.

I settled in to the routine pretty quickly. The major problem for me was working out what the time was, for example when was the time for going down to the laundry. This is a big thing when you are limited in what you can do. A few housekeeping issues were the major ones I had. That was all. I didn't have any great difficulties at all. Then people were coming in looking for information. I was getting material together to a certain extent for the full court hearing and other matters. Bit by bit I was getting some of my papers and material that I needed.

The various court appearances were a bit of a break but then I'm an odd character – I would have been as happy to stay in so that my routine wouldn't be disrupted. That just happens to be the way I am. But it was great for us at the same time. We'd come to court and meet people who you didn't know from Adam. You didn't know if you ever saw them before, but you knew from their response to you that they had been there and that they were out on the streets, that they were working for you. We noticed a big change with the reporters as well. I remember the second time we were brought to court an RTE reporter asking something when we were going back to the van and she was looking at us as if we were a strange animal. This changed. We were very much acceptable after a while. I remember one particular chat with a reporter. I said to him that I'm so well looked after now I expect to be much better looked after when I get home. And it was published!

WHAT HAPPENED AT THE RELEASE?

MICHEÁL It surprises me when I think back on the release. We knew there were discussions going on between the legal teams that we hadn't any input into at all. We knew that Shell was dying to get us out of jail and that the government was dying to get us out of jail. They were in a really bad way. It had finally struck the authorities outside that we were not in jail in order to get out of jail. We had to make sure that there was no confusion on this point particularly with the 'Free the Rossport Five' campaign outside which was the only campaign that realistically could have been run. But we had no input into it at all. It could have made it seem as if we were in jail to get out of jail whereas in actual fact we could have got out of jail easily, we could have just said okay and apologised. Even our legal people were quite anxious that one of us would get out so that we would have access to the High Court or Supreme Court. But we said no, if we do that we destroy the confidence of the people outside. It was obvious that we had to be careful not to start thinking that we were in jail in order to be got out of jail. The Taoiseach, back from holidays, announced 'they've made their point, they can come out.' No clue, the poor man.

We knew that Shell were desperate to get us out. Jerry Cowley came into us on the Thursday afternoon and said to us that they want you out. He said that they're going to go in to court tomorrow and they're going to ask to raise the injunction. I remember there was no real excitement. We said fine. I still remember it as very, very strange. The five of us were there. There was no burst of excitement. Then he said of course because you're being left out now the government wants you to take part in the Advantica safety review. And I said go out now and tell them that if they want to lift the injunction let them lift the injunction but we will have no more messing, we've put up with enough messing. We were more determined then and we knew about the support that was there among the people outside.

I'd been saying again and again, just joking, we'd say to the lads inside if we go out no one will talk to us! Our people don't want us out at all, they want us in here! The prisoners couldn't understand this. They couldn't understand at the start especially that we wouldn't just go out. We were in for the long haul.

Jerry was glad in a way that we weren't coming out so that they couldn't say that we had signed up to something or that it couldn't appear in public as if we've agreed to something. Anyway, about an hour and a half or two hours later he phoned and one of the warders came down for me to go to the office to the phone. And he said, you're out tomorrow with no preconditions. I said to the two warders that we are to get out tomorrow and they were delighted.

I was very low-key. I went back then to the other four lads. The warders were very strict about the prisoners going into each others cells. I said to the warders that I had to talk to the lads inside. One of the warders came in with me and I said, we're back in court tomorrow and Shell will lift the injunction so we are going to be released. We said we'd have to pack up our stuff and be ready. I asked the warders what do we do and they said have your stuff packed and it will all be shifted down. So I put the books for the library aside and I put my own books into a couple of boxes and packed up everything. And we had everything ready, nice and handy for the next day.

But our release was not straightforward which I found very disappointing for I believed that mostly people can find with goodwill a way out of an issue. When we went into the court our lawyers called us aside and said you're getting out, the injunction will not exist after today. You do not have to purge your contempt because there is no contempt in law, not now. You don't have to apologise but it would be a great gesture of goodwill if you allowed me to say that you did not wish to inconvenience the courts in any way, that you are the people that you are and that you are sorry for upsetting the court. So we said fine. He did this and Judge Finnegan threw it back in his face.

When we did get out meeting people outside was great. Coming out was a great buzz of course. We had to get ready for the media but it wasn't the media at all really. It was the people around. There was such obvious goodwill and delight. Outside the Four Courts in the rain Dan Healy and Maura Garvey played 'A Nation Once Again' as the crowds sparkled with excitement.

CAITLÍN It was amazing that day.

MICHEÁL On the way into the court the warders had the radio on low. We were just chatting away. There was no euphoria at that stage because we weren't yet out. Somehow it was still just part of the routine. The radio was just barely on and I heard someone mention 'my cousin Mike'. That was surely me! I asked them to turn it up. It was Marion Sheedy Kingston from Tipperary town, my first cousin! And she was giving out, I remember that. It was great!

We made an immediate decision then that we had to go back

home as soon as we could. We had to do the Late Late Show and RTE put us up at the Radisson hotel that night for the programme. But first of all we had to go for a cup of coffee! A phone call came from Seán Ó hEalaí, father-figure of local radio in Mayo, who said to me 'it's a tribute to the power of local media'. I agree with him absolutely. Without the freedom exercised by local media things may have been different. One of the dangers now is that local media is being taken over by major corporations and otherwise intimidated.

The kick on being released was wonderful. There was so much obvious goodwill. One of the other prisoners who had been out of jail before us had jumped up on the back of a Statoil lorry as it passed by and we had a photograph. He was so delighted. He was there and he was in great form.

After the rally in Dublin the next day on Saturday we headed for home. Everything was organised for us. We didn't have any input. We were still really freewheeling on other people's organisation. When we came into Mayo we stopped at Gerry Murray's pub in Charlestown. He had supported us through the summer. There was a pile of people there from Ballina and Castlebar. That shocked me. It was then I really realised that the world had changed. We were treated like Jesus Christ coming into Jerusalem! In Charlestown I knew that things were different, that the world was changed. We had been so busy up till then that things weren't clear. It was obvious, especially there. We had to go back up then to Dublin for a concert.

CAITLÍN There was a welcome home meeting in Ballinaboy at one o'clock and we had to be in Dublin for half eight.

MICHEÁL On the way up to the concert we stopped at a Texaco petrol station outside Swinford. A young lad of about eight came out and he looked at us and turned around and he ran in and his mum came out. He said, 'you're one of the Rossport Five' and I said, I am and he ran in and checked the photograph in the Connaught Telegraph and said 'Yes, it's him, it's him! Wait until I tell them in school!' Going over the Shannon we stopped at a restaurant and the mother of the owner stopped to congratulate us as we were going in. Inside people kept on coming over to the table saying we admire you, you're doing tremendous work, you're doing it for us. The same theme – the theme continued on – 'you're doing it for us.'

But it was on the way down, with the kind of solid, not very demonstrative reception in Charlestown that I knew the world had changed. Of course the welcome in Ballinaboy was crazy. People were so tremendous. Next day as well we were there. The world had changed then and I believe it is a different Ireland. It has remained changed. Yesterday, I was in Mitchelstown in Cork in a Tesco shop. A woman came over and said excuse me, are you one of the men who went to jail against Shell. We started chatting and she was saying how much she admired us. This is a year on.

I know this area will be destroyed if Shell's project comes through. The future of this area will be gone. I don't make any distinction between area and people or between people and environment. I don't see any sense in the area without people. There is continuity there from the Bronze Age or even earlier. To see that continuity destroyed for the sake of forty or fifty years. It affects me. For something so trivial as more money for already rich people.

I think even were we to lose this battle there has still been such a huge victory in awakening people. When we went into jail it was an absolutely unbelievable thing to do. But then all of a sudden thousands of people throughout the country found that they could do the same thing. And they can. And they know it. You would normally have a class thing or a social thing about going to jail among the super-respectable people. They haven't a problem with it at all. The people know there is hope. If we can succeed in doing what we have done then they have hope. I remember speaking to a senior civil servant from the Department of Energy a few years ago. When he retired early he didn't take any documents with him at all because he was so sure then that those in power had everything sewn up. He was sure that there was no hope of the people getting control of the country again because those with money and influence had sewn it up so tightly. But that's no longer necessarily true, I think.

CAITLÍN When the Dunquin field was announced off Kerry the people there said we will not let it happen like Mayo.

MICHEÁL Maybe it's because of the widening of significance of our campaign that has made what we're doing more realistic. Because it definitely wasn't a realistic thing last June to go to jail. I didn't see any hope at that time. There is now a national solidarity to this around the issues of fair play, justice and of giving away our assets.

CAITLÍN I think giving away our assets is crucial.

MICHEÁL But it's more than giving away our assets. Giving away our assets is also tied up now to notions of fair play. This is what gives me such hope I think. There is an element of idealism tied on to the money issue as well.

CAITLÍN And respect for people and for communities. During the summer I was very strong. There was a time when I'd have thought that if that happened I'd have fallen apart but I didn't. I thought it would go on and on but I knew it would have to come to an end sometime. I thought they'd probably have to purge their contempt. We are both old age pensioners and every day is precious, especially at that age in your life. I would think another week! I didn't find it too difficult going to the prison. It was tiring. What I did find very difficult was having to deal with the media.

When I came back after he was first put into prison my phone couldn't take more messages there were so many of them. There was a huge stack of post from people I had never met, from people I had known over the years through the Irish language, and from people I had taught. I couldn't believe it.

I didn't expect the end. I was saying to myself that because of the great support we had I knew it would be brought up in the Dáil. I was wondering would they be able to take the heat of that. It was giving me some hope that the pressure would come on Shell and the government. But apart from that I just didn't know when they'd come out or how long they'd be in. I didn't know anything. I got a call the night before saying that the men might be released. I was over in my daughter's house. I had planned to go to Dublin the next day anyway and instead I went up that night with another daughter. I rang each of the children then.

MICHEÁL When we were in jail I used to say to the others that there is no way we can get out of here unless Shell lift the injunction. That was the reality of it and I couldn't see Shell lifting the injunction. I couldn't envisage it happening. I couldn't see them doing it because of the enormity of giving in to the five of us without us even demanding it. It was something new. So it must have been a terrible blow to Shell because they had to lift the injunction. They cannot be sure of anything since then. Now, I can't see what Shell can do unless they do what we told them back in 2001 – go back to the drawing board.

CAITLÍN When they went into jail I believe that Shell and indeed our government who were backing them thought 'we'd put them into jail, we'll get on with the work, and when the work is done we'll let them out'.

MICHEÁL What type of Ireland do we want? This is why people of so many different political ideologies are very comfortable in this campaign. Because what it's dealing with is the context – the context is the big thing, the important thing, what should be the important thing, for everyone. And the context is what kind of Ireland do we want? What kind of Ireland do we want for the people after us, what kind of Ireland do we want to leave? Do we want to leave it to a new landlord grouping that the next generation or the generation after that are going to have to get rid of? Do we want to leave a legacy after us that can only be solved by violence? To me this is all about context. The people realise that the politicians will have to come back and function within a context that's real. And the context is what kind of Ireland do we want and not what kind of Ireland is most convenient for making money at a particular time. It's not awfully relevant whether it's for multinationals or for Irish companies.

I couldn't see Shell giving in last summer. They had never done it so I couldn't see them possibly doing it. They must know by now that their old system of working has lost credibility even in their own shareholders' eyes when they had to give in on this to a small group here. They know now that they are dependent on the muscle of the State to get this project in and the State doesn't seem inclined at the moment to use muscle. They were in Nigeria at one stage, and in various other places, but it looks as if that stage is gone. Shell's first efforts since the 1990s to pretend to become more environmentally aware ended with the hanging of Ken Sara Wiwo and his people.

Their whole effort here has failed too because they cannot do it within the context of the corporate culture they have practised. The only thing they can do now I believe is to seriously look at what has happened with us and to establish an entirely new approach based on what they would have to do to deal with us here. They would have to acquire an entirely new corporate culture before they could get the Corrib project in.

I don't know if that is possible. The Shell leaders can say well, we did it once when we let them out of jail. That was a very destructive thing to do to our corporate practice and culture. Maybe if they come to projects now on the basis that the natural resources are not owned by governments but that they are owned by people then maybe they could advance. But otherwise I cannot see how they can advance or what they can do. The only way they can get this project in is by using the power of the police because it is not acceptable to the community here. I don't believe they can do it.

CAITLÍN Even more people locally have come on board to get Shell out. If this ever came in the whole place is going to be changed forever. Our way of life which is expressed in the stories and the placenames and all of that.

MICHEÁL People here do not have a dogmatic approach to belief. They are very much aware that we do not control reality but that reality is something we share. Reality is what enables us to function now at this particular time.

CAITLÍN There is a local prophesy in a story that says a wave will rise at Glengad and sweep up the estuary. Now we believe that refers to gas. That story comes from a huge number of people all over the area.

MICHEÁL People will still tell you locally that the last battle from some prophecy or other will be the battle of Ballinaboy. To me this is an echo of the awareness of people back to the Bronze Age time. An awareness that having a grip on a place is tenuous and can be destroyed. You can have an evil god like Balor who can destroy the thing and a Lugh Airgeadlámh isn't always at hand.

CHAPTER 3

'You cannot buy safety and you cannot buy happiness'

Philip and Maureen McGrath

BACKGROUND

PHILIP I'm the youngest of twelve children. I had a lot to live up to! My father died when I was eleven so we had a hard time growing up. I went to England for about ten years and returned in 1990. That's when I met Maureen. My mother was sick at the time. She only lived for two years after that. Being the youngest I suppose you were always the favourite. Whether it be a boy or girl the youngest is always the favourite. Though sometimes you wouldn't admit it yourself!

You were glad to get away when you got away but when you came back it's then that you appreciated what you had. You almost have to leave home to appreciate it. I was mostly in London. I was mini-cabbing there. It was a busy lifestyle but it kept me out of the pubs! I also worked in Yorkshire for a while. I found Yorkshire to be very close in a way to Ireland. Even the people were very Irish in their ways. People who you did not even know would ask you how was your day's work. They were a really friendly people. I think it's then it started to grip onto me. The community spirit there reminded me of home.

It was about a year after going to Yorkshire that I came back. Of course when you come back you see what you've been

missing – the shore here, the sea beside you. You can walk out
onto the shore anytime and have a bucket of mussels, cockles.
You'd never have that there. That's what I missed, I think. Just
the country life. In particular fishing. I was mad for fishing. I'd
fish day and night. I was glad I came back. I'm glad today.
Sometimes I used to say to Micheál in prison (he was our
teacher in school), I wished I listened to you instead of looking
out the window in school. I should have been listening to you!
Then I wouldn't be here today! He'd turn around and say, well
aren't you better that you are here today. And I am. Probably if
I'd more education I wouldn't be here today. But I'm happy
enough. It's very close knit here. I've lots of relations about.
Nearly everyone's a second cousin! I've three brothers about
here. The others are in London.

MAUREEN I'm from Portacloy, five miles from Rossport. I'm
the second one in the family. There are three more sisters and
a brother. I never went away from home. I never really wanted to.
I worked in the knitwear factory in Ceathrú Thaidgh. Then I
worked in the hotel in Belmullet for a while which was nice too.
I had no yearning to go away. I was a home-bird all the time. My
mother never went away. Just two of my aunts went to England.
None of my family ever went away. They were all married around
home. I have a sister married four miles from here, and another
sister married in Bangor Erris. The eldest sister is married in
Maynooth. She married a local man. He's a teacher. My brother
is at home. He's the youngest one. He does the farming. My
father died while Philip was in prison. He had been ill for about
six years so it wasn't easy. We miss him all the time. I'm near
them so at least I can give help. I gave a lot of help when my
father was sick.

Where I came from there was always scenery around me.
There was the bay there too. So I was used to that. My father
used to fish. When he was young he caught one of the biggest
salmon ever. That was in 1949 – 1950. Thirty-five pounds
weight! It was only broken last year I think. He made his full
season of salmon that time on that salmon alone. That was from
a currach.

We have such scenery here in Rossport. When you come back
you appreciate it. The same after you had to go to Dublin. I
rarely went to Dublin other than now and again to see my sister

and maybe to do some shopping! When Philip was in jail we used to have to travel to Dublin. The weather was so warm during that time going to Dublin. When we arrived I couldn't believe how you couldn't get fresh air there. I felt claustrophobic. At least here you can go out on the warmest day of the year and you can get a bit of a breeze. You can look out on the sea.

Like Philip I have lots of cousins around here and various relatives. We're all very close here.

PHILIP Everybody knows everybody. Sometimes they know too much! That's the downside of the country, everybody knows you. It's good to go away and then when you come back you appreciate it. No matter how long someone has been away when they come back they see all these things they missed. A lot of the people are coming back today from England. A lot of them for their old age.

MAUREEN The quality of life here is about scenery but also the quietness and the peace. You haven't got the traffic compared to Dublin or all those other cities.

PHILIP We are different in a way from other parts of the country. I suppose this place here was unique in its way. It was probably the last part of Ireland that was untouched until we were chosen by Shell. But before that nobody had ever heard of Rossport. People wanted to know where it was close to. They'd say, Rossport, is that near Westport? They always knew Westport. But today when you say Rossport it's a different story altogether. They jump up now when they hear Rossport.

MAUREEN We got married in 1992. We are quite settled here now.

WHAT WAS YOUR FIRST WORD ABOUT GAS?

PHILIP We were living here in Rossport of course. The first we heard about the gas was in 2000. There was a lot of talk and there was something in the local pub about it. But, when there were questions raised they didn't have answers. They were fobbing off. Then a man came visiting all of the houses. He had all this paperwork with him. He was telling us that all that was happening was that there was this gas pipe coming in. It will be good for the area. There will be money and jobs. I suppose nobody really knew much about it.

MAUREEN We believed in them at the same time.

PHILIP We believed in them because all we ever knew was that there were gas pipes going everywhere, from Bord Gais and that. That's what he was telling us.

MAUREEN We didn't know the difference at that stage. We didn't understand the danger.

PHILIP They came and told us about this three-stage payment. You'd get half first, then you'd get the other two-quarters when the pipe goes down and is finished off. So for people who were only getting a thousand euros it wasn't a lot of money over three years. At that time they hoped to be pumping gas in 2003. (It's 2006 and there is still no gas. And in 2026 there will still be no gas through Rossport!)

Everybody knew that there were these fellows from Enterprise Oil at the time calling to the village. After a couple of weeks visiting people and telling them about digging trial holes they came with the papers and said, just sign here. You'd have your money within three weeks. And it was very tempting of course. We were offered a nice amount ourselves. Of course it would have paid for a lot of things.

However, we started to query it then a bit. I think he came again. I asked him something about safety, something about distance. There was something I had seen about a gas accident, in the News of the World I think.

Oh, he said, that's not my department. 'I don't know anything about that'. So he was only there to fill in papers. And I said well, come again and you might tell us about that before we sign papers. Six years later I haven't seen him since. You see, they knew nothing and it's the same today.

WHY DID YOU HAVE DOUBTS ABOUT THE GAS PROJECT?

PHILIP It was probably something I had been reading in the paper about a refinery somewhere. It might have been about an explosion and distance. I had read that the distance should be over a hundred metres anyway. I was just asking him about this and he didn't have the answer. But he said, 'I'll send somebody back to you'. To this day they've never come.

MAUREEN The pipe was only to be 70 metres away from our home.

PHILIP That's why I asked him that I had seen something about a hundred metres. He didn't know anything about it. What he said was 'you shouldn't have to worry about that, there was no danger'. Right from the start I had some inkling against the thing. They were talking about this as an ordinary pipe. There was no information about this being a pipe with raw gas. We thought it was going to be like what they have in Dublin or Meath and other places. At the beginning they had tried to bring it in on the other side of Sruhwaddaccon Bay.

Most of our neighbours had signed but we hadn't. I don't quite know what was happening at that time. Maureen was sick then. She had two operations. I fizzled out of it. I took a back seat really in the first year or so. I didn't get involved in this until about two years ago. So many people used to say to me, oh you have taken your money. I used to say, what money? Then when it came out a couple of months after that that I hadn't signed they believed it.

I suppose what I was worried about was that it was too close to the house. They said it would be fenced off and that you could never run the tractor over it to cut your grass or anything like that. That was worrying in itself. To think that you had this part of your field where you could never walk with your cows. You'd nearly have to get permission to drive your cows over it. This kind of crazy stuff.

At the beginning we were all acting on our own. There was nothing worked out. Willie said to me at one time well, I'm going to have to go to jail. I said to him, that's great! Then after a while we thought we'd have to stand up no matter what. I said, yes, I'll stand with you. I used to joke with him, 'if you're first and the judge puts the hammer down on you, I'll walk away then'!

MAUREEN When Shell started coming around to the houses they came to us and used to say, 'if you don't sign we'll bring you to court'.

PHILIP They used to say, we'll get compulsory acquisition on you anyways. Naturally, for people who did sign, the mention of court was a big threat. We never knew anything about court and neither did they. It was enough to frighten anybody. That's why a lot of them probably signed, they were frightened not to. For us it didn't matter at that stage. Because at that time they were coming digging trial holes anywhere it fancied them. They'd have one in your garden if we allowed them.

MAUREEN They dug a few trial holes in our fields all right but that was as far as it went for us.

PHILIP We got a few pounds for that. I said to them 'you can dig the trial holes but you'll never get my signature.'
They were calling regularly to the house. They were telling us about the good features of the whole thing and safety. They were saying how there would be work there, and you'd be near home. They said, 'we'll get work for you.' Several times the fellows came and we still didn't sign after that.
We were more aware then of the pipeline pressure and those matters. That was about three years ago. Micheál used to be on about the pressure and how unique it was. The Ballinaboy people were going on about the terminal at the time too. Shell was never talking about pressure. They did say there would be 345 bar pressure going through it but what was that to us?

MAUREEN We didn't know much about the refinery either. We thought it was an ordinary building. As we went along we were learning.

PHILIP Because there's no such thing around anywhere. You wouldn't know unless you were really in to it. You'd have to have been a real bookworm to figure out what it was about.
Many people were for it at the time in this village. One reason was that Shell was visiting them all the time. They were constantly brainwashed. Also, the older people were brainwashed from the Church. The Church had done that to them. The local parish priest at the time was important in getting the gas as far as it got. Himself and the bishop went out onto the gas rig offshore and they blessed it! There was a big flare burning there and even the priest couldn't see that here

was the priest on one side and there was the devil on the other side! All the early information was coming from the Church. How it was good for the area, how there would be jobs and we would get gas.

The older people followed the Church. What the priest would say, in the school, you would have to do it. The older generation is so religious and pious that if the priest said it is OK then it is OK. But the views here have changed an awful lot about the project. People now are starting to sit up and realise what is coming. They see now the dangers. About what would happen if there was an explosion. For example, if the pipe had been in at the time of the landslide [In September 2003 a series of bogslides occurred on Dooncarton hill overlooking the proposed gas pipeline landfall point.] the village might have been wiped out overnight. They say it's only time before there's another landslide. Think of what would have happened if that pipe had been in! Some of the rainfall cut into the ground more than thirty feet deep. More information has been got out. Also the power of the Church is slipping away now. They ruled everything, the schools and so on. All through the years. But it is coming out now how the Church abused their power.

During the visits that we got from Shell it was always about 'we'll get you work there'. It was always about work. 'Wouldn't it be nice to be working at home'? I wasn't working then so it would have been nice. I had only done some building work for three months for a local fellow. 'It'd be nice to get back into work', they said, 'we'll sort it out'. 'You'd never know in the long-term we might get you work in the terminal'. That is what they were feeding me. I suppose they were saying this to everyone who signed, that they'd fix them up with work. It was a kind of blackmail. Another fellow came from Cork at one time with paperwork and the offer of money. 'We want to give you an extra bit if you sign early'. 'If you sign within the next twenty-one days we'll give you an extra three hundred' or something like that.

With us, the atmosphere with them when they visited I would describe as slimy or slithery. They were trying to get into your heart. 'This is the right way'. This was the Shell attitude always, whether they were Enterprise or Shell, they were the same faces. They all went to the same school of training.

Later they used to be writing us letters saying they were going to attempt to get on our land some day.

MAUREEN I'm glad to say that we didn't sign and if we had signed we would have to backtrack over the signing.

WHY WERE YOU SO DETERMINED?

PHILIP As I said before I had spotted something about safety. There was just something about it. It was something new for the area. When I raised it with the first fellow who called they never came back on it.

I used talk about it a bit with Willie. Myself and Willie were always close. Our mothers and fathers before us were very close too. At the beginning nobody was really into any great depth in conversation about safety. But we were saying that something is wrong here. Why pick us here for this project? Nothing ever comes to the West that's any good. So why come to us with this? This was spurring us on to find out what was going on. We were looking at all their plans and so on. But we discovered in time that everything had been signed away. All the rights had been signed away by government ministers. Probably there were brown envelopes passing, maybe ten years before. Nobody can prove it of course. Now was the time to call in the favours when the money was spent.

WHAT HAPPENED WHEN THE COMPULSORY ACQUISITION ORDERS CAME?

PHILIP They got some ex-guard in Ballina to deliver them. That came about two years ago. First of all we were frightened. This was it! We had to read through it. I was never one for reading a book. We read through it without really understanding what it meant. We couldn't get a solicitor to represent us. It was impossible. Once they heard it was against Shell they didn't want to know. Myself and Mary Corduff went to one solicitor in Castlebar. He charged us €600 for an hour and a half and then he wanted €10,000 up front to show the case to a barrister. We ended up representing ourselves. Then we got a solicitor in Ballinrobe. He represented us for a while but then turned his back on us. He was doing the usual thing of taking us to one side in court and asking us would we settle with Shell. It showed that Shell was operating according to money behind it all. They were always wanting to settle the case with us.

When we got the Acquisition Orders it spurred us on even more. When they had gone to this stage with us we could not turn back. We probably had more temper against them then. A bit of anger was getting up then.

But there was the same level of support in the village. The CAOs didn't change that. We were pretty isolated really at that stage. There was a lot of finger pointing. That we were stopping the gas and stopping progress. People were saying to us why are we holding up the gas. Any place we'd go we'd meet some fellow – he might not have been from the area at all – and he would say, 'you're the ones that are holding up the gas'. We'd say but this is dirty, raw gas and they'd say, sure it's the same all over Ireland. 'And I'm working on gas in England for forty years and not a word of it.'

It was a lot of pressure on us. People were saying, sure they know about gas and you know nothing about it. They were so convinced by what they were reading and the propaganda that was coming out from Shell. Shell was all PR all the time out before the public eye.

Even at that as I said we weren't too involved before the last couple of years because of Maureen's health.

MAUREEN It all came down to stress.

PHILIP It was all from this. She had inflammations in the stomach and then gall bladder problems. It was the pressure.

MAUREEN I suppose we didn't realise that it was that that was causing it. But today I do realise that it was the gas, that it was from all this that was going on. Because I was such a happy person, I was such a happy person before that. Then I started to get sick. I couldn't find out what was wrong with me. I ended up having to go privately down to Galway to consultants. At one stage they had to take out my appendix. I had to have an operation. I was only back home a few months when I started to get sick again and next thing it was my gall bladder. So I spent many months not able to work or to do anything. I missed out on my social life. My father was also sick at that stage so I had to attend to him. I don't regret it but I'm a bit angry that I wasn't able, with the pressure, to spend more time with him. Especially when later on, a year ago, with Philip in prison, I wasn't able to give much time either.

PHILIP The pressure was still affecting us.

MAUREEN It was there on our shoulders all the time but we didn't realise it. We were always afraid of the word 'court'. What we would think is that they could take your house or your land.

PHILIP You could be criticised as well any time you went to the pub. We've always said that we've been very lucky between the five of us who went to prison that we wouldn't drink a gallon of beer between us for the whole year.

If we did drink much you wouldn't be able to sit in the pub and listen to some of what was being said without arguing back. It was constant abuse. I took a lot of it. I suppose I was the one going to the pub! They'd say you're the one holding up the gas, holding up progress. Those people didn't want to hear the truth. An old neighbour of ours used to say that the truth is bitter and he was so right.

MAUREEN It was great when Vincent became involved, just to have that extra person. And Micheál was behind us too all the way.

PHILIP With Vincent from the village too and living along the proposed pipeline it was a big help.

WHAT WAS GIVING YOU THE COURAGE TO STAND UP?

MAUREEN The danger of the pipe.

PHILIP If it came in we'd have to leave. When you set up a home it is very hard either to pull out or to be pushed out. For us, we were not choosing to pull out, we were going to be pushed out.

Something you had built up. When you have a nice home and a comfortable home you had everything like what we have around the house, flowers and a lawn. You'd have to leave that behind. I would have had to leave.

MAUREEN For me I wouldn't want to leave but I suppose if it came to it I would have to leave. Philip used always say, 'would I leave' but I would always say no, I couldn't leave because I love the area so much that I couldn't live in a town. But if it came to it I'd have to go but I would miss the area very much. If I was away from my family I'd feel really isolated.

PHILIP Like anyone who would have to leave their home after being pushed out there would be heartbreak.

MAUREEN The heartbreak would be terrible.

PHILIP People have been thrown out and evicted all over the world and many die of heartbreak overnight.

WHAT WAS IT LIKE WHEN SHELL STARTED COMING ONTO THE LAND?

PHILIP They used to write to us saying they would be coming onto your land on such a day.

MAUREEN Sometimes they used to come without telling us if they were in the area.

PHILIP We'd spot the jeeps around. You'd have to be on your guard. That's how it was. You had to be around your house twenty-four hours a day. You had to be there all the time. You'd be watching about for these jeeps. All of a sudden, they could call up to your land and try to get in with no warning. They did that with Willie a couple of times. For example, one day it happened in Willie's and we had all gone out to the field. The guards were there then. We said, that's it, we won't see them again. So, later, I was out in the garden doing shrubs. I was watching lots of activity back on the road. There were a lot of jeeps. 'There's something happening here', I thought. Then three jeeps pulled over all of a sudden on the side of my land. I just took off running.

I got onto the mobile straight away to Willie and said to him they're at my house, come over. I was running trying to get to the fields. There were about twelve men there. The guards were there too, parked in on the side of the road. This is in early 2005. A few months before we went to jail. Probably in March.

When I reached them I said, 'hold it, where are you going?' They said we have been writing to you. That's a lie, I said, you have been writing to my wife, nobody has been writing to me. Another fellow with them said, you look like a reasonable sort of a man. They said, that was a mistake, maybe we have been writing to her all the time. I said, you're coming on to my land with no paperwork or anything, writing only to my wife. I said there's something wrong there. 'You look like a reasonable man, maybe we can sort something out', they said. I was so desperate for time, I said well, I suppose we could. I said a million should cover it nicely! And they said, 'well we can sort something out'. I ran then for the gate when I saw Willie coming and said, well I've changed my mind. He thought he had me. Could you imagine? I said one million!

MAUREEN Then the support came to the gate.

PHILIP But imagine the way they reacted to it!

MAUREEN You'd say what you had to with all that crowd from Shell surrounding you. The guards were just parked in at the road at that stage.

PHILIP They always looked to me as the one they could buy. I don't know why. They always used to say that to us. I suppose we were the only ones that were keeping up a conversation with them compared with the others. Yet we might be the toughest in the end! They always thought that they could buy us. Certainly from that time with the million when they said 'well, we can work something out'. You see how they reacted to it. In Shell's world money buys everything but not us.

They said we want to come on to the land to peg it out. I said I want to see your paperwork. They said we have consent and we don't have to show it to you. I said you have to show it to me. Are you obstructing, they said? No, I'm not, I said. I had my hands in my pockets going over and back before them! It was so strange. So then they walked away. They started to peg on a right of way that was there. Three of them had stayed back to do this. I said no, that's my land, I own both sides of this so I claim the road. We didn't see them again for another three weeks. Then they made a last attempt. That day they tried everybody.

MAUREEN The weather was so wet that day.

PHILIP They had the injunction at that stage. Maureen was just after the operation then. They were all parked outside the house.

MAUREEN On that day I had just come from the doctor.

PHILIP There was a lot of media there that day too, from Mid-West Radio and TG4. So there was an awful lot of stress around. Even when I came along I could feel the stress already. It was unbelievable really. Maureen was the one that was suffering. The rest of us could go out and talk about it and get rid of it. But for the person that's there and can't move, they take it all in to themselves.

MAUREEN I was always looking out for them to arrive. At one stage when they attempted to get into the fields I happened to see them passing by. Philip was up in the bog. They had come from trying our next door neighbour's house. I just rang him and I told him. You couldn't go anyplace without your mobile phone. You had to be contacted if they were ever trying to enter. So I just rang him on the bog from the house here. He came down running.

PHILIP They were always saying to me, 'why don't we have a chat'? This was to me. This was the attitude to me. So they always took it for granted that they could buy us. I don't know for what reason.

MAUREEN I suppose it was just that we were more polite with them throughout. Which we shouldn't have been. I went out during these attempts and I told them to get away, get off the land. I was getting bitter against them at that stage. They were haunting us. They were annoying us and they were messing up our lives. You couldn't go to Belmullet or Ballina at any time. You'd have to ask someone to watch out for them.

PHILIP You were always on guard. We thought they would try and get on as soon as we were gone. You were always on duty but you weren't getting paid for it! It was like security round the clock.

Once the injunction was got we were in a different situation. We were heading for the courts now. We went up to the injunction hearings. They swore at the hearings that Willie had assaulted them. The judge believed it! How could the judge have believed that? I think it's how they are so naïve.

The injunction was served by paper on us. The same fellow came as before with the CAOs. Everyone came together then in a meeting in one of the houses. It was straightforward – it was straight ahead. There was nothing else we could do. We were putting everything on the line, risking everything. You were risking losing your house. It could now be taken from you rather than you just being pushed out which we were facing before. The pressure was there. There were some nights we couldn't sleep, roaming around the house all night. You just had to keep going and put the risk out of your mind and say that if we don't fight them they're going to come in and push us out. Maureen is the one with the guts!

MAUREEN I was determined.

PHILIP I was never really an aggressive person. But if I did blow up that'd be it! I'd be mad for a couple of days.

MAUREEN We were putting all that we had on the line. The campaign was getting harder and harder all the time. But then, it came to the point when we stopped the lorry on the road from coming in to their compound in Rossport. They were bringing plastic pipes into it.

The rest had been in Dublin just that day at a court case. Vincent was the first one that came on the scene where the lorry was coming in the road. So the word went all around to give support. The lorry was stuck there for about ten days or two weeks. We were out there night and day all the time.

PHILIP There were nights I went out there at two o'clock in the morning. You'd just sit there in the car. That was before the lorry got blocked. We were keeping an eye on whether there were lorries coming down late at night to supply the compound. One night I thought they'd be no one else out at such a time but at three o'clock Willie sat into the car with me. You see there was nobody sleeping at that stage. You were on twenty four-hour guard because they were running things at night. Even with the injunction we had to stick with it. Whether it was courage or desperation! Desperation.

To test the injunction then they went into our neighbour's field. She let them peg so much of it and then they stopped then. That was the day I was on the bog. I came down then to them from the bog.

Again they said we should have a little chat. Another one like the last day. So I knew I had to waste time because I didn't have help the same day. So we had a chat. I went over to the guards and I said to them have you your handcuffs today. They said what would we need handcuffs for. I said if you don't use them today you'll never use them. 'Oh no, there's nothing to do with handcuffs.'

MAUREEN Shell tried all the fields that day of the people who were against the pipeline.

PHILIP When he came to my field and was stopped the Shell man said to me, 'I'm sorry that it's come to this. You know it's court after this'. I said, 'I do, whatever it takes'. I think behind it all that was the only time some of them showed to me they had a heart. They probably thought that I was their last hope and here I was stopping them. I knew we were heading for the courts.

MAUREEN They tried a few the first day and then came back the next day and tried Brendan and Willie. It was raining. After trying Willie's field they gave up then. It was court after that.

PHILIP All the names were taken of anyone who had stood on the land. Young and old. But the only names that came out for committal were the five men. All of Brendan's family was there, and Willie's family, myself and Maureen, all of Vincent's, and others. You're talking about thirty, maybe thirty-five people. We were thinking we were all going to be up in court. We thought we were all going to be jailed. There were some tense times. After that then we had the lorry incident in the meantime.

Before that the Good Friday walk showed that there was support. There were a few hundred there. It was surprising really that so many people even thought about it. We didn't realise that kind of support was there for us. When we saw that we said well, there's something here. There's something worth fighting for. I suppose it helped us a lot getting through, that all these people were behind us.

But as I've said the negative from others was always there. There are so many people that do not know how to be anything else but negative. They would never know how to be positive.

BEFORE YOU GOT TO THE COURT FOR BREACHING THE INJUNCTION, CAN YOU EXPLAIN ABOUT BLOCKING THE LORRY?

PHILIP In the lead-up to it there were a couple of days where we had blocked them from going in to the compound. If anything I was the first one involved in this. One evening I saw three lorries coming in. They had pipes on them. There were flagmen about but to us we didn't recognise them because they didn't have any authority. So I drove out past a flagman and I stopped on the road. But the lorries kept coming towards me. The road wasn't wide enough even for two cars without one being in the ditch. The drivers came up to me and said you have to reverse. I said I can't reverse. Well then, you have to pull in, they said. At this time other cars were starting to arrive. So I said, why don't you reverse? He said we can't, we might go into a drain.

So we all got out and had a chat. There was a bit of blinding going on! Some head fellow came from Shell who told us he was in charge. He was fairly thick with us. They're used to dealing with people in blunt ways. He said he would have to phone the police. They came and said do you want to be arrested? We said, that's fine. The guard walked into the Shell compound and was gone for about an hour. He came back and asked us if we had made up our minds to let them pass. We said we hadn't. They then sent for the superintendent. So the superintendent came along. Eventually we struck a deal that they could come in to the compound, turn their lorries around and head out. There were a couple of Shell supporters there watching the lorries come in despite us. But the lorries came and turned and went out. That was victory for us. I said that's Big Tom's song! They're going out the way they came in! Their supporters were really shocked. They knew from then on that they were going to be under pressure. Now that we had struck once. This was our victory for the first time. The first time we had got to turn them around.

After that they had a local man bringing in pipes. So we said that this will have to be stopped. There was no traffic plan, for example. On one day a phone call came from Glenamoy saying there was a lorry coming full of pipes. So Vincent met it on the road and there wasn't room for it to pass. Everybody joined in then. It sat there solid for two weeks. There were lots of names taken there as well.

There were good crowds there. Different people altogether getting involved in it. People were more coming on board at this stage. I think it was because we were starting to stand up and be heard. At this time, Shell were beginning to shift the bog in Ballinaboy but people saw that we were standing up and being heard so people from Glenamoy started to get involved. Once they got the edge on it then that was the spur to get them involved. We were sleeping down there at night. It was rough going.

MAUREEN The weather was really bad. It was raining most of the time. All the work on the farm was being neglected. There was nothing done. It was night and day shift. They used to go out and come in. They might have a quick sleep and go out again. That's the way it was going on for two solid weeks.

PHILIP The lorry was blocked to make a point that this is it, that we draw the line here. We just did not want any more Shell material coming in here. There was no way we were allowing the steel pipes get in because it would be the end if they got those in. At that stage they had started to peel back the land just beside the compound.

We thought that it was now definite that they were ready to start. We believed that if even they got one in they would start welding. So the line was drawn then – that was it. Fighting them like this was both stressful and good.

MAUREEN I suppose I didn't mind the pressure at that stage. You had no time to think.

PHILIP You were dealing with them face to face because they had to come and talk to us. The only time we ever talked directly to Shell was on the road.

WHAT HAPPENED AT THE COURT AND PRISON?

PHILIP I remember the night before the court it was very emotional. We were out on the road and people were saying goodbye, good luck. You knew that you were going and probably were not coming back. You had that gut feeling.

MAUREEN You went for a pint to your local.

PHILIP They were all out on the road as I was leaving the pub. The shivers went down my back. I couldn't sleep. I slept a bit on the bus going up the next morning. We knew what we were facing. We had the gut feeling that we weren't coming back. We went with the intention of not coming back. It was frightening though, not knowing what was going to happen.

In the courts the case was being moved from room to room. Then all of a sudden it was brought up. They were going to deal with it on the day. I looked around and we had no solicitor present. 'Who has all the papers,' I asked? We went up before Justice Finnegan. He told us that he could take everything off us. We were given time to think. Then we were sent into the same court later before Justice McManamen. I remember going in and Brid McGarry was beside me and she said, 'I stand to lose everything.' Well, I said, at this stage we just have to keep going. We thought he was going to take everything. I was the first one to be called. There was no running! I was smiling at Willie beside me because I had told him as I said that if he got done first I'd run then. But it was me up first! The judge asked would I continue to obstruct Shell. I said I had no choice. I had to stand in front of them because I didn't want to be a guinea pig. And he went through the others then.

I knew by the look on the judge's face that he didn't want to do it. He said he had no choice but to commit us to jail for contempt of court. That feeling then that we were going to jail! My legs were jelly. I always say it reminds me of the Tom and Jerry cartoon where Tom gets the hammer on his head and the legs start to crumble first and the rest of him starts to go down all the way.

Then the guards came over and said, 'this one'. That's when it gets you. You get the tap on the shoulder, 'come on'. They let us there for some time with the family and friends in the court.

MAUREEN I was at the truck on the road. When I heard I just fell to the ground. I was so upset. I started roaring and crying. Everyone was in shock at that stage. They couldn't believe it. We were trying to ring up to Dublin.

PHILIP It had to be an awful shock to everyone. All over Ireland even. The people in the court, the barristers and solicitors, they couldn't believe what was going on. We were there in the hallway and there was an awful buzz out there. When we did leave the court there were people crying. They were all in a frenzy, I'd say. I never saw so many cameras in my life. They were gone berserk.

When we got into the Bridewell we kissed goodbye to the daylight! Even though we knew what we would get, reality is a different thing. The sentence is a different thing altogether. What does anyone ever know about prison except what they see on television? You were always thinking it was possible that Shell might drop the injunction at the last minute. That it wouldn't go ahead. But instead of that! I suppose it was up to us at the end of the day. They wanted us to apologise. Even Shell's lawyers were white in the face. They were all shocked. They knew that it was the wrong thing that was done.

As soon as they brought us into the Bridewell they told us to hand over our phones. They brought us upstairs into a big concrete cold cell. There was an echo there that would blow your head apart. There was a high ceiling. There was a small little window with a couple of bars over it. We were there talking for a while. I suppose we were largely in shock. A couple of us lay down on the concrete slab there and fell asleep for two hours or so. Then they came in and gave us tea, a breakfast roll and a Mars bar. They said this'll keep you going for now. They were asking what were we doing there. They couldn't believe it when we told them. Where was your solicitor, they asked? I said he's at home. He never turned up.

Then they said they were bringing us out to Mountjoy. We were taken in the dog-box! It was quite an experience. It was a tiny little space for each of us. Then the steel door slammed. As we were going off we could still hear the people outside. I could hear one person we knew shouting, 'its scandalous'! I could hear them in the distance all shouting. They were all cheering. We got then to Mountjoy. The holding area we were brought to was all dark grey and rotten. We were brought in and these big doors closed. They took all our watches off us, our money was all counted out. We had to sign for everything. Just as they were taking us away the phone rang. A change of plan, we were going to Cloverhill. They said to us you're not going here after all, you're lucky, it's bad here, it's not a place for you. There are the real McCoys in here! So we went out into the yard. The first man we met was a prison officer from our area! He told us Mountjoy was very bad.

We were then taken off to Cloverhill. We couldn't think where it was. The brain wasn't working at all. Again when we left Mountjoy they were all shouting outside the gates in support. Cheering for us. We were heading into some place where we'd never been and never dreamt we'd be. When we went into Cloverhill then we were brought into a nice colourful area. We thought it wasn't like prison at all. There were tiles on the floors. They told us to sit down and that it would be a while before they'd get to us. They offered us a cup of tea. They took our photographs.

We were all then assigned cells. I suppose we were there about an hour and a half. It was about half nine when they gave us our cells. We were in Cell Number AI 13. My prison number was 35996. On July 17th Maureen and I were thirteen years married. So cell 13 – that number was unlucky for me! They brought us into the cells and gave us a bit of food there, some cereal. They said that it would be best for us to stick together when we go out into the yard in the morning.

We had to dress the bed then. Once we hit the bunk we were flat out. Before that we had to change into the prison uniforms. That was the most humiliating part of all. We had to strip off. You were handed a towel. That was it. You walked through a screen. They searched all your clothes and your pockets. Once we hit the bed we were gone.

The doors opened at ten past eight and it was hard to get us up then. We hadn't slept really for two or three weeks. Next morning when we woke up the governor came to see us. One of the nuns who worked there had come in to see us straight away that first night. She was very good to us. It was around ten o'clock at night and nobody's around at that time.

MAUREEN They were very good to the wives at home that

night. They managed to ring us.

PHILIP She came and asked about us. She asked are they ringing your wives.

MAUREEN The prison had to get the mobile numbers of the wives so we could be contacted when they were taken in.

PHILIP So she got all the contact numbers and she rang each one telling them that we were fine. That first night we just got on with it. I suppose we were still in shock. But the next morning we were told that the best thing would be to stick together when we were out in the yard. 'There are a lot of people out there and they mightn't like you because you're from the country.' So we went out into the yard. As soon as we went out they all rushed towards us. I said this is it, we're all going to be killed! But they stopped and asked what are you doing in here. It was all over the news before we came in at all and in the morning it was on the television.

MAUREEN The media was all in Rossport the following morning.

PHILIP It was something to keep the prisoners going. They wanted to know why were we there and how come someone who was innocent could be in there. They were all taken by it. So we got on great. They were very interested. I suppose it was something new for all of them for innocent people to be in. You'd find out though the little things they were put in for – no insurance, no tax. Many were in prison because they had no money to pay for tax or insurance. They were thrown in there for a spell. One man was put in jail for drinking a pint bottle of Guinness in the Phoenix Park – just to clean the city up for tourists, I suppose. The younger Dubliners there used to call us the farmers. There were a lot of travellers there.

One prisoner told me he had been transferred from Mountjoy to Cloverhill. He said it was so bad in Mountjoy that he would listen to the suicide squad late at night. I didn't know what he meant. He said the cockroaches were so big that they would climb onto the ceilings and drop onto the floor.

After a few days they got the sense of where we were from. One fellow said that his uncle used to sell shoes in Rossport. From Ballymun to Rossport! They were good to us and they were looking out for us. We got a lot of advice from them like if there was a fight they would say to keep your head down because if they see you looking you might be next!

Even when we went out to get our dinner, I remember there was this Scottish fellow who became a very good friend of mine. He used to be on the serve. He'd be serving maybe the dessert – jelly and cream or something – he'd put out a big scoop and say, 'solidarity, mate!' Just what you needed – double helpings! There were all these fellows in for their own thing but they were still able to know that ours was wrong.

They'd listen to us on the media. It was on every station. We had the television in the cell and the television used to hold some of the radio stations. You had 106 fm. All through the nights – some nights when I couldn't sleep – I'd be listening to this. They were on about the Rossport Five constantly. These were stations in Dublin. You'd wonder how in Dublin it would take on so big.

We weren't frightened by the other prisoners. Of course some you might be wary of. There were always a few looking for cigarettes, always looking for something.

We had to register then with the governor to get a phone card. From that you had a number, a code. You would stick that in and you'd get a six-minute phone call each day. If anything went wrong during the call, if it got cut off, that was it. You had only one chance.

MAUREEN We were always waiting for the phone call.

PHILIP Sometimes if I couldn't get Maureen I would tell Willie to tell Mary that I tried to phone. It was hard. The six minutes wasn't enough. Then we started to get visits. I got the odd box visits.

MAUREEN I found it very hard going to the prison. He was there for two weeks before I went to see him. My sister went to see him first. She was on holidays at that stage in Cyprus when they were put in. But it was two weeks before I could face it.

When the court decision was announced he rang me at the lorry. 'We are going to jail', he said. I just fell to the ground crying. People were very good to me on the road. They had their hands around me and they were very sympathetic to me. People offered that night to stay with me. Anything they could do for me they would. I stayed at home that night and I stayed on my own. It wasn't easy. All the time they were in prison I stayed here on my own. People offered to stay with me. I said I'd prefer to stay on my own because if I stayed in someone else's house I'd just make a habit of it. I wanted to come back to my own house.

I thought at first it would be a few weeks. I thought they'd be let out again, that something would happen and that Shell would lift their injunction and let them out of jail.

The phone calls were coming once a day. You wouldn't get much chance to talk. We used to have to write down what we were going to say to them on the phone.

PHILIP The calls were all recorded as well.

MAUREEN You could easily be cut off. You'd have to wait for the next morning or the evening to see who the next phone call would be from.

PHILIP We tried to regulate it among ourselves that one of us would ring in the morning and one in the middle of the day and one in the evening.

MAUREEN The men were always giving information to each other. The wives then, we would always be meeting in each other's houses. It was great. There was so much going on with media. The rallies started then. They started just a week after them being put in jail. There were huge crowds. The first rally was in Castlebar. There was a huge crowd there. That's when the real supporters came out. That's when we believed we had the real supporters behind us.

I started then going up to see Philip. My brother-in-law used to go up with me. I couldn't face going on my own. I used to have to leave the house at five o'clock in the morning and travel to Dublin. We had breakfast on the way up. We'd be there around half past nine. We'd stand there at the door of the prison. The queue then would start to come in with other visitors. The door wouldn't be opened until ten o'clock. You'd go up then to the counter and say you were here to visit Philip McGrath. You were given a number. You'd sit there and have a cup of tea or something to eat. The next thing your number would be called.

The thing I found most hard was going through the gates. When one was opened another would be locked. I found that very, very hard. The first time I went I found it genuinely hard. After going there a few times we got used to it. We used get some box visits which wasn't too bad. The time you had was fifteen minutes. We used to head off then home and we were shattered by the time we'd get home. There was always something happening the following day again. That kept going on all the time. It was hard on the men but it was just as hard on us, the wives.

PHILIP I think it was harder on them because they had to be there for everything.

MAUREEN We were going and going all the time. We didn't know we were going so much. To rallies and all that. In the evenings we all had to meet and be around for this one and that one. We were getting a bit strong at that stage as it went on. We didn't know really what we were doing. We were just going along every day as it was coming. When we look back now you'd say would I ever be able to go through that again.

PHILIP You just had to drive on and that was it. It was very emotional to see her on the other side of the screen. You could not touch her.

MAUREEN My sister was the first one that went up to see him before I went up. We kept going up then for the visits. It was hard. There was nothing easy about it. At the time we were under so much strain and stress but we didn't know it. We just kept going and going. We knew at that stage they weren't going to come out in a few weeks. As the weeks were passing we knew they weren't just going to come out. Shell wanted them to apologise to the judge. We knew that they wouldn't apologise.

PHILIP We went through the silly season at that time. Judge Finnegan had said there would be a judge always on duty if we wanted to apologise. I always remember that. 'They'll always be a judge available.'

After about a week we were eating and feasting really. We said we'd want to cop ourselves on here or we'll end up like barrels. We might be in yet for a while.

MAUREEN I found it very hard in the beginning.

PHILIP The third week was my turning point.

MAUREEN When I used go up I'd say don't give in. Don't apologise. I used be telling him about the support out there. How we were at the rallies and about the numbers of those ringing us and all that. They could never see the support that was there because they were inside. We were on the outside and we could see it.

PHILIP You have to tell how it was. It was hard. On the third week that was a turning point for me. We might have slept for two weeks and then on the third week we woke up. I found it really hard. I was down in the dumps. On one day I was so down the guard left me in rather than making me go out into the yard. Everybody was supposed to go out. Come on with me, he said. He told me he was from the country. 'We wouldn't want anything to happen to you. My mother would never let me live it down!' He brought me up to see the doctor. He said, this fellow is very down in himself. Then after that we went in to see the psychologist. I had a chat with the psychologist. It was great. He said, I'll see you again next week. This was it – it was an hour once a week then. He said maybe if you had something to do, it would be better for you. Let's go down and have a word with the nurses. So we went down and she said would you like a job? She said if you had a job cleaning or something it would be better for you because we know ourselves this is not your place being in here. She said how would you like the kitchen? She said leave it with me and I'll see what I can do. This was on a Saturday morning. On Saturday evening a man came to the door and said I hear you're looking for a bit of work in the kitchen. So I went down with him and he showed me around and he asked me what did I think. I can't wait, I said. Pick me up, I said, half eight in the morning. So I went in and started work. From that day I never looked back. It was the turning point.

On the outside people have no idea what it's like in prison. One thing I learned was to say nothing about what you see or hear. There are things you take for granted outside like being able to walk on the shore or go fishing. There are certain colours that cannot be worn like blue tracksuits or shirts. The prison wardens have to be always addressed as Officer or Miss. A Sunday in jail was no different from any other day. I was approached once to bring in drugs. The inmates thought that I wasn't searched as often as they would be. I told him I came in here innocent and I intend going out the same. There was a mesh roof over the exercise yard to stop drugs being thrown into the yard.

MAUREEN It was funny when I used go up to visit him. First of all he was dressed in his green uniform and the next thing he was in his white uniform! I didn't believe it.

PHILIP In the mornings the doors would open at ten past eight. The first turn they'd give to the door – it was like a double lock – was at six. Then at ten past eight it would turn the second time. Everyone had to go out and get the cereal, the rice crispies or cornflakes. You were brought back in again. Everything was eaten in the cell. That was the hard bit too because you'd have over in Mountjoy a common eating area. Everyone has a table to sit in. Here everybody had to go into the cell.

Then you were locked up again and the doors would open at half past nine. You had to clean out your cell. You washed the floors and everything and swept out. You might get to the shop then before ten o' clock. Out to the yard then until a quarter to twelve. They'd bring you back in at five to twelve. They'd do a count. Then they'd open the doors and you'd go for your dinner. No tray, no dinner! If you didn't have a tray you didn't get a dinner.

You had to have your shirt always buttoned up. If you had your shirt open you could be sent back and not get anything. They had a strict dress code. You got your dinner and went back again and were locked up until half past two. Out again until a quarter to four. Again they'd bring you in then and have a count. You'd have your tea at four. At a quarter to five they'd let you out for the last time in the evening. You were out until about ten past seven. That was a long spell.

There was nothing there other than to walk around the yard or read the paper, or smoke a few cigarettes. I went on the cigarettes when I was in. I wonder why! You came in then from the yard and got out to get milk. They locked you up then at twenty past seven. That was it. You were there until ten past eight the next morning. That was the longest time. I had awful trouble sleeping. I'd be walking around the cell.

MAUREEN I suppose obviously pressure.

PHILIP You'd be able to walk down to the kitchen at home. But several nights in prison I woke and jumped out of the bed and I was at the door! In three or five steps. Nowhere to go. I'd put on the kettle or put on the television. The boys would be sleeping – two trains going each way! A train going south and a train going north! They wouldn't hear a thing. I'd be there all night. I couldn't sleep at all.

We used to get some newspapers every day. What we'd miss on the newspapers the other inmates would hand us and say there's something there in that newspaper. They were very good like that. They'd push the paper in under the door.

The kitchen was a new life. I became the washer. There were all bambarees there, no delph. The bambarees were handy for washing. No steel knives or forks either. The food was cooked in trays and turned into the bambarees with the lid on. They were served from them. There were just paper plates. Whatever you wanted to eat there you could eat. Of course you never had any ham or beef, the nice stuff that you really liked! Anything that was on the menu and left over after it was served you could have. You had vegetarians and vegans. There was always food. If you wanted fish or rice – all these different diets were there.

The first day we came we had the Dublin coddle. I'll never forget it as long as I live. For the Dublin people it's a great dish but not to us. The only thing I could eat out of it was the bacon. The sausages were like hot dogs.

I was in the kitchen all day long, from half past eight to half past five. I got three euro and twenty-five cent per day. One time though we got a bonus – one coke, one tayto and two chocolate bars each! A ten-year old child would expect more. It was the full day in the kitchen other than if I got a visitor. Then you'd go to Mass on Sunday. There was always a big crowd there. All the different wings of the prison were together.

Jerry Cowley was a hero to us. He used come in constantly to visit. You wouldn't go to see your best friend as often.

The first week we were in we were getting the odd card addressed to Mountjoy. We were supposed to go there at first. They were sent over to us. Then the cards started to really come. Just ordinary letters and cards, not the pre-made 'Shell cards'. They hadn't started coming at the beginning. We were into the second or third week when the mail started to really come. The officer would come up to us with this bundle. We'd say is that for the wing. He'd say, 'that's for you. So help yourself.' We'd divide it up half and half and pass it over the next day.

One day I saw him coming up the hall with this big bag. He had a long face on him. We said what's wrong with you today. What do you think, he said. A bad day, we said. Oh, a bad day all right, he said. 'Do you see what's in the bag?' So we looked in. It was all filled with letters and cards. It's all yours, he said. I've been sitting at a computer all morning, he says, registering every single one of them. He said, you have as much post here as the whole prison would get in a year. In one day, imagine. Who else gets letters in a prison? One person in particular, Pauline, was a star. How she got the mind to write as much? She used send a letter to each of us in turn every couple of days. She definitely had two letters coming every week. We'd see it in the bag and say, that's from her. It was great because she was keeping us up to date. She'd have snippets from the papers. It was mighty. Without her, myself and Willie used say, we'd never know anything that was going on. Because you couldn't get enough of time on the phone. We used circulate that letter among us.

We knew then there was a big change on the ground. You could see it even in the prisoners. They'd come up and ask how were we doing. We'd never seen them before. They'd say, my mother and everyone are not using Shell or Statoil stations any more. The same sense came from the prison officers as well. They stopped filling up at Shell and Statoil. One told us that he was out one day heading west and his car was jumping. He was nearly out of petrol. He passed a Shell garage and he almost went in. But he didn't. I felt so good, he said, filling up at a Maxol. He did that, he said, because of what they did to you.

We were broadening horizons. I suppose we were bringing more people on board. Explaining things. These were probably government supporters there who had never read anything about it other than from the Irish Independent. There was nobody buying the Irish Times there until we started getting it. It was the Independent only. When I'd get the Times in the kitchen they'd all swipe it.

MAUREEN We used bring up the Western People to them every week.

PHILIP In the kitchen you had the washing of course. But there were other jobs like the cereal had to be packed into a bag. You're talking about 400 prisoners and they all had to have cereal in the morning, so 400 had to be packed that day. You had tea, sugar, and salt all to be put into bags.

I saw how it was in the prison system though I wasn't there that long. You fall into a routine and it's very hard to get out of it. I'm not surprised that people that come out of prison after being there for long reoffend because they cannot live the life outside. They have to go back. That did happen there. We were there three months and we saw people returning. Within the three months they were back again. They would say to us we're back and you're still here! They couldn't understand it.

You were getting into it. You were looking forward to your day in the kitchen. As long as you did x amount of work everybody was happy. There was one Russian fellow there. He was in for murder. I was frightened at first being in the kitchen with him with all the knives! I said how come they let you I here. It's okay my friend, he joked, I killed him with my bare hands!

In the kitchen you'd wash the floor twice each day and everything had to be cleaned. Everything was pulled apart for cleaning. You wouldn't see such standards in hotels. It was the second year running they had won the top hygiene award for the jails. You could bring back some food to the cell at night, but never glass, tin cans or plastic knives. Some of them during the day might have made pies. There was always something different. One of the officers came in one day and said are you opening up a shop?

Sometimes after all your good work in the kitchen, as I said earlier, they'd give you a bonus of sweets. For grown men! How downgrading is that?

WHAT WAS THE RELEASE LIKE?

MAUREEN My father died in the meantime on the 18th of September.

PHILIP I had this thing inside of me because my own father died when I was only eleven years old. Maureen's father was a kind of father figure to me. I was very close to him. Though we couldn't look at each other most times when I'd be doing something for him, we'd be arguing about it, yet we'd come in laughing. I was always afraid something would happen while I was in jail. I said that by any means I want to be there at the funeral. At first the governor told me the only way was that I'd have to purge my contempt. It went on like that for a bit trying to find a way. I was told that there was a van outside ready to take me to the courts to purge my contempt. Anyway, something emerged and I didn't have to. I don't quite know under what provision – something about compassionate leave.

I got out in the evening of the 19th at about half past five. They gave me my money and the mobile phone. They asked me was it charged and I said, I don't know because I couldn't think of the pin number! I was so long without it that I couldn't think of the pin number. They asked me how I was going to go home. I said the train, I suppose. They said was there anyone picking you up. I said, no. So they said we'll drop you down. But it was half five and the train was to leave at ten to six.

We'll get a man to bring you to the station, they said. I got my money and the money for the train ticket. They said to the man dropping me that if you don't make Hueston you have to bring that man down to Mayo tonight! We'll make Hueston, he said, come on. He put on the sirens straight away and off we went through the traffic. We got into the station about a quarter to six. But after queuing to get the ticket we had to run to get the train. He opened the door for me and said, goodbye and good luck. That was it. I thought somebody would have to come with me.

MAUREEN I expected that a prison warder would come down with him and that he would just have a few hours.

PHILIP I thought I would just get out for the funeral and that would be it. There was a man on the train and we were talking about rapeseed and oil. He kept looking at me. I kept the head down. I was frightened of the media, of course. I got picked up then at Ballina. But at the funeral I was afraid some of the papers would arrive and turn a private thing into something else.

MAUREEN I couldn't believe it when you did walk into my parents' house.

PHILIP I didn't know where I was. I had travelled all that distance. I was in there for over an hour before it just dawned on me where I was. When I went in they were asking did I want tea or anything. I said no. It took me a long time to get settled.

When we headed home that night I sat into my car but I was so nervous driving. The steering wheel seemed massive like a truck's. When I came back to our own house here I stood outside the door waiting for the door to be opened. I guess I was falling in to a routine. The door always been opened for you. I would always have opened the door for a woman. But there I found myself waiting for Maureen to open the door. I came in the door and the colours hit me. The brightness. I had to turn down the light, the dimmer, because I couldn't see where I was going. The brightness. I couldn't sleep then. The bed was too comfortable.

So the next day there were all these people who came to the funeral. In the church people came up to us before the Mass. The priest at the ceremony welcomed Philip here from the Rossport Five.

It was a big boost to see the support. We went to the pub then after the funeral and I just sat down at a table way down in the corner and never moved. It wasn't the place when I was in jail to be drinking and mixing. An awful lot of the people were there to give support on the gas as well. That's when I knew the support was so high.

MAUREEN Even though we were always telling them about the great support the funeral told it all.

PHILIP You got the feeling there of the support.

MAUREEN And the way the people shook your hand.

PHILIP There was a grip there. The grip was killing me altogether. They'd shake your hand but with the other hand grip you and say, well done, keep it up. The next morning I had to head back. Someone asked me how are you getting back. I said I was catching the train. He said, no the media will be waiting for you and asking the wrong questions. So he offered to drive me all the way back. As we were going there was a crowd gathered in Glenamoy early in the morning. That was something. That was what you call emotional. That's when I really did see it. We were in Ballina before I could speak. It had really gone through me.

MAUREEN It was hard on me seeing him going off. I didn't even get the chance to mourn my father. He died, Philip came home and then he was gone again.

PHILIP There were thirty or forty people up in Glenamoy that morning, clapping and whistling. It put the shivers up my back. When I got back to the prison I had to wait for about an hour for them to get the papers organised. They weren't expecting me back! They must have thought that when they let me off that would be it. That I would definitely apologise. Some of the officers told me they had a little bet among themselves that I wouldn't return to jail! The prisoners said to me why didn't you stay out! But when I got back in the other men were all around me getting the news and I was able to tell them about the support. After that it all started to happen. Within a week or so we were out. But being let out didn't hit me or affect me as much as it did them. I already had had a taste of being outside.

I was in the prison shop two days before we got out. I asked them when would they be getting the Christmas cards in. They looked at each other surprised. I said book me two boxes.

It was Thursday night, September 29th, that the news came that we might be released the next day. I was a bit sad to leave because I had met some nice people there who were innocent. I tidied up a bit. On the eve of a previous court appearance I had cut my ear lobe while shaving. It started bleeding and wouldn't stop. They put on paper stitches and a bandage around my head which looked like the Easter bonnet. So I was careful that morning!

When we were getting out the media attention was like something you never imagined. The media that was outside that day was like for film stars. I never thought I'd see the day when photographers would fight over me for a photograph! We had got word the night before that there might be something happening, that we might get out.

Then I thought, will I get a chance to say goodbye to the fellows in the kitchen. It's strange to say – I say it and people think I'm mad – but I was a bit sorry too. Because you had got into a routine. It was like you were starting a new life. It wouldn't be a life of course I'd recommend but you had got used to it. And you had made friends there. And there wasn't a chance to say goodbye to them.

When I came home I didn't have the routine to get up at half past eight and head off. There was something missing. You were used to having a full day.

In court the judge kept going on about the apology. During the hearing we expected to be going back in. He wanted to put us back because we didn't apologise for the contempt. He wasn't happy that day with us. Even at the end of it we didn't know whether we could go free or not. When we went out into the Hall, the circle, it was a frenzy. We were told RTE was looking for us. When we went outside it was mad. The flashes of cameras and stand here and stand there. It was madness. You were back in it again. You had had the London bombing which was serious but you still had the Rossport Five. We held the attention all the time.

I think people connected with us because they were afraid this could happen anywhere. It wasn't just something happening out in the country. This was about a private company who, if they wanted a piece of land, they could get it no matter what you did. If they wanted something at the back of your house they could get it if this law goes through. People realised that this could happen anywhere.

MAUREEN The rally the next day in Dublin was unbelievable really. There must have been easily 5,000 there. That's again when it hit you.

PHILIP That's when it hit us. When we got up on stage and saw all these people. If there was a politician brought into the Dáil he wouldn't have that level of support.

MAUREEN We travelled down then home after the rally on the Saturday. There were bonfires from when we came to Crossmolina. We stopped first in Charlestown, in Gerry Murray's pub. There was a nice crowd there. Then we went on to Crossmolina. The people were all out from there.

PHILIP Mid-West Radio was covering it. They aired it all the way. There were bonfires all over, in Crossmolina, Bangor, all around. In Ballinaboy there was a great crowd. Different people now who were coming out. You would never think they were involved in this at all. That's when we got the real support – the real support was out for us then at the homecoming. You had people there who you'd never have expected. It put a different light on everything. It was a great feeling. You had the crowds and the bonfire. Micheál was at the front of the bus all excited. 'And this is all for us', he was saying. He was right.

As soon as we left Bangor I really felt it. It was clear the mood had changed around completely. People knew we didn't go to jail without something being wrong. There had to be something wrong for five men to go to jail. It had taken them a long time but they were seeing it now in a different light. That support has stayed solid and has grown.

There is no hope here for Shell now. I don't think there is any scope for anything for Shell any more. Hopefully there will never be a terminal up there in Ballinaboy. As long as we go on fighting there will be no terminal. At the end of the day a terminal is going to be as dangerous as a pipe. The pipe is dangerous but if they get the terminal there it's worse.

My brother-in-law was here from Iran recently. He was saying you don't see in Iran refineries or terminals for miles. They are put away from people into the deserts where they don't affect anybody. By the time the fumes have come out of them they are gone. He said it's madness putting a terminal in the middle of people.

I came back fairly well after prison. I didn't think I would. I was afraid that I might have difficulties coming back. The littlest things. You might have the dirtiest job to do on the farm and you'd never do it. But today I would do it and look back on it and say wasn't that lovely.

MAUREEN So much work was being neglected for the whole summer. This year now we've been so busy in the garden and that shows what was not being done. The solidarity camp people used come in the summer and help with the garden. That was great. They used to take the pressure off me. They'd help out like with taking turf home from the bog. Philip's busy all the time now and you'd say where was all that work done last year.

I had my own routine too and then he was back home. Especially after he had gone back to prison in the week or so before I didn't expect him home. We were really shocked when we heard they were getting out but at the same time we didn't know was it really going to happen. But if we had to keep going on we would have kept going on. As long as they would be in jail we'd have kept going ourselves. I would face into it again if I had to.

I feel so strong about it. It's for our health and safety and our own home. If we had to leave here in the morning how could we start all over again?

PHILIP You can't put a price on that. You cannot buy safety and you cannot buy happiness. If you are happy and content somewhere you cannot buy it. I am more determined now than ever before.

MAUREEN We expected them to be in for Christmas.

PHILIP They used to tell us when we were there after a month that Christmas dinner is not bad! You'll get a fry in the morning and a nice bit of dinner with something to drink then with your dinner. A glass of wine or cider. With a nice bit of turkey. It's not bad. As the time was going on we were getting closer to that. I'd say to them, is the dinner still on for Christmas and they'd say yes!

MAUREEN At the first anniversary of their imprisonment there was great support. At Michael Davitt's grave they laid a wreath and then we came back to Ballinaboy and there was again a great crowd.

PHILIP One result of our experience is that I look differently on people elsewhere who are fighting for causes. Before I wouldn't have taken any notice really. All we can do now though is to offer our support. Various campaigns now all want one of us to come along and be there with them even if you don't say anything. Just be there as a booster.

I was always Fine Gael to the backbone. When Enda Kenny ran here in his first election I sat in the polling booth for him. Today now I look back and I say how stupid I was doing that. Just to think that he has turned his back on us. I have said it to him. What can we do, he said, our hands are tied. I told him that I feel ashamed that I supported him after what he did to us.

I think Ireland as a whole is upside down. I don't think there is any rule there at all. We always used to say 'Shell county council' but Shell is ruling the country on this.

People probably thought we had all cracked up after coming out of jail. The first day or so after coming back I was out there in my shirt in the pouring rain. It was lovely. I think it was one of the best things. I was out in the rain and I loved it. When you were locked in there, there was a kind of wire mesh over the yard to keep out the drugs being thrown in. It was like artificial sunlight that was coming in. You weren't getting the full ray of the sun. You were more inclined to be stuck into the shade. We were in Cloverhill in the middle of the city. Having the mesh over us there was twice the heat, with us trying to breathe.

I do resent Shell. I would anyone who did what they did to us. They say now, oh we'll forget it and start over. But you can't. I'm good-humoured towards the jail all the time because wherever I'd be I'd try and make the best of it. If you work at something and you're not happy leave it. So I made myself happy there and content. And I was happy enough.

MAUREEN Of course I am bitter towards Shell. After what they did. We had a really hard year last year. But we're still going to fight on. We're still going to stand. If they have to go back to jail again they'll have to do it.

PHILIP At the end of the day it's our land and nobody else's. Not Shell's. I think it will come back to a conflict again and the next time it will be more serious. It won't be just us. I could see us in the firing line again but the next time they will be giving a sentence. They made a big mistake putting us into jail from the point of view of the PR they got. But they had tried everything else up to that and it wasn't working.

MAUREEN The trailer and pickets at Ballinaboy are there over a year now. The support is great. Thousands have signed petitions. We'll just keep on going. The trailer stays until the end!

CHAPTER 4

The onward struggle for justice

Brendan Philbin

BEGINNINGS

In 1996 Enterprise Oil discovered natural gas in the Slyne Basin which was located 70km off the north Mayo coastline in the Atlantic sea. There was a consortium of various oil companies involved in this venture with Enterprise Oil as operator of the development as they possessed the largest shareholding of 45%, followed by Statoil at 36.5%, and Marathon Oil at 18.5% respectfully. As a result of this discovery it was decided on and proposed in 2000 by the developers and the powers that be, that the unprocessed gas would be brought ashore and purified at an inland terminal/refinery to be located at Ballinaboy in the townland of Bellagelly South, Ballina, County Mayo. This location as proposed was to be located within a mature conifer forest covering hundreds of acres of ground and owned by Coillte Teoranta (the forestry board). The site was located on top of a hill and was surrounded by Carramore Lake on one side which was and is the main drinking source for potable water for the people of Erris, (currently with a general population of 10,000 inhabitants) and Sruth Mhada Conn estuary (which has historic relevance with respect to the Children of Lir) and its river tributaries which included the Glenamoy river (a key salmonid river) on the other. As the site drained into the lake and the marine environment which were both candidate SACs and/or SPA status under European legislation any works carried out on site would have a detrimental impact on the integrity of these sites with respect to the Habitats Directive 92/43/EEC and 79/409/EEC respectively.

I expressed disbelief at the time that that site would be chosen as the land was peaty in nature and bog-based imbibing 90% on average of held water, was 15-20 feet deep in places underlain with "dóib" (a dense quicksand-like substance with highly unusual characteristics not yet properly understood) and was located on a flood plain. These ingredients made up a recipe for disaster and in the original application the material in question was intended to be excavated to form a footprint covering 20 hectares and terraced among conifers on the side of a hill surrounded by these waterways in an area of heavy rainfall. The whole concept beggared belief. Could the developers be serious? And what of the state agencies? Would they respond to this environmental lunacy in a very sensitive location (as time progressed it became blatantly obvious that they would not respond in an adequate fashion)? At the time that these motions were being put in place little did I realise that myself and my family's lives would become entangled with the oil business, the State and other development groups acting as key players in orchestrating the total destruction of our pristine area.

We were made aware in our community of the potential benefits which would accrue to the local economy in the form of jobs and a supply of natural gas to our homes. These soundings were expressed and communicated via local radio and the local newspapers. The Minister for the Marine at that time, Frank Fahey, promised the moon and the stars from this find for the area, and most people lost the run of themselves thinking about the financial benefits which would be delivered to each man, woman, and child. It was all wishful thinking as the true revelations began to unfold as a deeper knowledge was kindled with respect to the overall project.

Enterprise Oil and the consortium's plans consisted of the connection of seven subsea wells in the Corrib field to a manifold which would pump the unprocessed or raw gas ashore at full wellhead pressure, in this case 345bar (based on the developer's data) via a 9km pipeline to the proposed refinery site at Ballinaboy. The proposal was to route this pipeline through Broadhaven Bay which was and is a haven for whales and dolphins, and make landfall at Dooncarton (later to be become the focus of the national media's attention as a series of landslides occurred on the 19th September 2003 – Corrib gas was not mentioned however, even though the landfall for the unprecedented pipe complex was located directly beneath Dooncarton mountain). The land pipeline complex was then to traverse along the coastline on the Pullathomas side of the estuary. The overall operation connecting the refinery to the wells offshore was to be controlled via an umbilical tieback. This control was to be operated from the proposed Ballinaboy site via a complex umbilical system at a pressure of 610bar delivering hydraulic fluids offshore to the wells.

There was also a proposal for an effluent discharge pipe in the same trench which would contain chemical elements including mercury from the purification process on site and this was to be discharged off Erris Head within the catchment area for containment in Broadhaven Bay, in effect resulting in a local chemical sump area for the operators. The operators disputed this fact however and maintained that the effluent would discharge and dilute into open sea. Consultants on their behalf conducted biodegradable dye tests in the bay to assess the flow characteristics. In 2001, EEI were present in the Broadhaven Bay area and barges were dredging in preparation for laying the pipeline at the landfall. An amount of hydraulic oil was released and the fisheries board were notified. This oil washed up and is still present in the lower Glenamoy river to this day. Even though the relevant authorities were notified of same including Mayo County Council and the Department of the Marine no clean-up was ever initiated.

This once again was highly reflective of the apathy which the relevant State agencies displayed towards our pristine area. No party was held accountable for the spill. EEI refused to route the discharge pipe back to the wellhead where the location of gas seam cavities would contain same, thus minimising adverse effects on the marine environment. This was proven standard technology in the oil and gas industry which again reflected in a very negative manner the plans which were to be put in place in our area.

FIRST ENCOUNTERS

I became aware of a new development in August of 2000 when a representative of Enterprise Oil called to my residence and told me that the pipeline system would be going through my land. I was very surprised and shocked at this news as myself and my neighbours were of the opinion up to that point that the proposed route was to run along the Pullathomas side which was located directly across the estuary from the Rossport area. I began to realise at that point that this project was not being handled correctly as too many changes were being made in a very rapid fashion. It dawned on me that I would have to conduct extensive research into the overall proposal as it appeared from the series of events which had unfolded that a proper and thorough assessment of the area had not been carried out and thus it was only a matter of form for the developers to join (a) in this case the terminal/refinery to (b) the proposed pipeline route to be established. The representative informed me that the pipeline(s) would go through my land and expressed indifference at my concerns. I was also informed that they intended to conduct survey works for the new route in the area.

It later emerged that the route through the village of Rossport was to traverse from the landfall at Dooncarton across the Sruth Mhada Conn estuary (second strongest current in Ireland) to the Rossport cliff face, take a right angle and run through the village, onwards through Rossport South where myself and my family live and onwards through Sáilín on towards Ringmoir where there is a forestry plantation which is owned by the Mc Garry family. The pipeline then takes a sharp right turn across the bay into Lenamore heading towards the refinery at Ballinaboy. This route was detailed on a map supplied by Enterprise Oil as operator in the year 2000.

Enterprise Oil set up a few consultation meetings in the area for the landowners and residents to attend. I attended the meetings and expressed misgivings that this pipeline was not governed by Bord Gáis Éireann i.e. was not a transmission pipeline, and that I had genuine concerns about the refinery and the pollution effects and the peat removal issue to name but a few. However my pleadings were generally ignored. I also expressed the view that the people in the area were not against the processing of the natural gas as long as best available technology was used, such as off Kinsale in County Cork, which had been developed by Marathon Oil (partners in Corrib) in the 1970s and which was controlled and maintained on the mainland by Bord Gáis Éireann as a transmission pipeline in effect utilising clean odourised gas at reduced pressures of 80bar. I enquired and put forward basic questions to the representatives present which included engineers and other experts in their respective fields and they individually and collectively did not seem to have answers or understand our position.

A basic question which was put forward for their attention from the residents was the peat handling issue on site, and how it would be removed and stored in preparation for the refinery footprint. I also expressed concern about the removal of the peat along the proposed pipeline route and the stability of same as the engineers present stated that the pipeline would be buried one metre in depth. I was concerned about buckling and fatigue factors as the pressures involved were enormous when one considers that the pressure in a car tyre is 2bar. The peat-based soil was acidic in nature and did not have the same cohesive strength as regular mineral soil. What of the corrosion properties associated with this type of soil and its effect on the pipeline? Once again the representatives present did not appear to grasp our argument. As farmers and residents living in the area who utilised turf as our main source of domestic fuel we had gained an in-depth logical knowledge and experience from cutting turf for harvesting purposes and thus were highly aware that the developers would run into problems. They did not seem to appreciate the type of material they would have to work with from a handling point of view, not to mention the risk that the removal process would pose to the localised sensitive environment as the site was surrounded by rivers and streams. The engineers present outlined and kept confusing our argument about peat with the characteristics of gravel material. They explained that the peat would be handled in the same manner. At this early stage it was becoming very self-apparent by the minute that we had questions to ask but that unfortunately for us the developers had no answers. I felt very concerned and disillusioned about the overall development at this stage, and little did I know that the worst was yet to come.

In October of 2000 I received a phone call from Bríd Mc Garry who resided in the next village of Gortacragher. Bríd and her mother Teresa had expressed concern about the pollution effects from the proposed refinery and how it would impact on the residents of the area and the environment and they had taken a very cautious approach because Bríd had a scientific background and thus was very suspicious of the whole affair. She informed me that it had come to her attention that EEI representatives were on their lands. She told me that they had not been approached by EEI employees and as a result of this had decided to make further enquiries. Upon speaking with an employee of EEI, he stated to her that they had been on the lands and had conducted tests on the land in question which included a forestry plantation. She informed him that they were trespassing as they had not consulted with them about the pipeline route and that this was their private property. The employee stated that they had modified the route once again to include the forestry plantation and that it was their understanding that it belonged to Coillte (the Irish forestry board). Teresa asked for the letter that they had relied on stating it belonged to Coillte and to this day they have not received it from EEI. Bríd explained that herself, and her mother were very upset about the situation as it appeared that it was being handled in a very underhanded manner. It later emerged in April of 2001 during the height of the foot and mouth disease outbreak that a further trespass had occurred when the Mc Garry's encountered an employee of EEI once again on their lands, and he in turn informed them that the route was modified once more and that it was now going to go through all of their fields as well. The Mc Garry's were dumbfounded by the bizarre trail of events which had unfolded before them.

OPPOSITION

In November of 2000 a series of gas pipeline meetings were set up by the Irish Farmers Association (IFA) in Mayo. The first one I attended was held in Crossmolina and it was well attended. This meeting was intended to cover both the landowners affected by the Bord Gáis Éireann transmission pipeline route which was proposed to traverse from Ballinaboy to Craughwell in County Galway, and the EEI unprecedented upstream pipeline complex in the Rossport area. We were informed that the IFA had negotiated with EEI and that it had taken over a month to reach an agreement.

THE FINANCIAL PAYMENTS

1 Permanent 14m wayleave	€11.00 per linear metre
2 Crop loss and disturbance	€13.50 per linear metre
	for a 30m working strip
3 Early sign-up	€3.00 per linear metre
TOTAL	€27.50 per linear metre

The main conclusion from my attendance at these meetings was that the IFA after negotiating for over a month had come up with a package containing the exact same figures as for Bord Gáis Éireann. These figures were later modified to €18.00 for a 40m working strip which was what EEI stated they required. Myself and other landowners affected by EEI's proposal also attended a meeting in Carne Clubhouse in Belmullet where representatives of the IFA and EEI were present. We were told at that meeting that the IFA once again had conducted exhaustive meetings on our behalf and that they were suffering fatigue as they also had to deal with the BSE crisis. I knew at this stage that the IFA were instructed to impress on the landowners present that this was basically a Bord Gáis Éireann pipeline with a few minor modifications and that there was no real difference between them. We were told that 'we were getting money for old jam' by an employee of the company. Needless to say myself, and other landowners lost total respect for the IFA after the events which had unravelled before us. We were to be sold out for a pittance by an organisation who was supposed to represent us. Michael Davitt who had worked tirelessly on behalf of the Irish people in setting down the stepping stones for the foundation of the land league, and whom I greatly admired and respected and whose philosophy was that "the land of Ireland was for the people of Ireland", would be turning in his grave with disgust.

As our community were informed about the potential benefits which would accrue to the area and the State from this development I decided to find out as much information as I could with the assistance and tireless effort of other residents in the area. The information which we collated and grouped together was startling to say the least as it gave an overview into how the family silver i.e. our natural resources which represented billions in real terms were given away. This was a shocking revelation considering that Ireland had an enormous offshore territory with huge extraction potential for our country and this potential had been squandered away to private consortiums whose only remit was to supply the energy only if they wished to do so, and only to the highest bidder. We found that there were two major differences between events which occurred for the Kinsale Field off the Cork coastline which was developed in the 70's and what would occur with respect to the Corrib Field off the coastline of Mayo. In 1975 Justin Keating who was the Labour Minister for Industry & Commerce at the time introduced offshore exploration terms which included a tax rate of 50% on profits, a 50% stake automatically accruing to the State with respect to commercial finds and royalties of 6%. In the year 1987 this fundamentally changed when Ray Burke (who was established as a recipient of corrupt payments in the Flood tribunal) became the Minister for Energy. He abolished the 50% stake with respect to commercial finds, abolished the State participation, the royalties and also introduced a clause whereby any expenses incurred by the private companies could be written off against tax. These changes came into being in 1992. The Taoiseach, Bertie Ahern was the Minister for Finance in 1992, and under the Finance Act the corporation tax rate on oil and gas was reduced to 25% which was the lowest in the world. The exploration companies were able to write off their exploration and development costs resulting in a delay factor of years, even decades before any tax was accrued to the State.

This was damning information which meant that in effect the people of Mayo and Ireland would gain practically nothing from these riches in our oceans. To add insult to injury on acquiring this insight it would appear that the indigenous people of Erris were also to be sacrificed into the oily bargain with the environmental repercussions and the unanswered health and safety aspects associated with this ticking time bomb. To add even further insult to injury the Irish people were denied this colossal revenue which would have contributed enormously to the upkeep and maintenance of our hospitals, schools, roads and other relevant infrastructure.

PLANNING APPLICATION

On November 22, 2000 Enterprise Energy Ireland Limited (new Irish title for the consortium) lodged an application referred to as P00/2934 to the planning section of Mayo County Council for a gas terminal at Ballinaboy. Mayo County Council requested further information and subsequently the developers withdrew the application without comment. At this stage a wider group of concerned individuals had become aware of the health and safety and environmental concerns associated with this development and began to express an interest. This was the last thing that the developers wanted to occur as it was better for them that matters were kept low key. It appeared to me as if assurances were given at a higher level that there would be very little resistance with respect to their plans and that it was a done deal.

A second application referred to as P01/900 was submitted on April 30, 2001. The new application referred to a footprint site to be located 500m to the east of the original site as per the original application which was withdrawn due to deficiencies. Once again Mayo County Council requested further information from the applicant which was highly reflective of the complexities involved with respect to the planning process. At this stage I had become engrossed in reading the Environmental Impact Statement, which was composed of volumes of reading material. It was a very daunting task which required many hours of my time and effort as it was important to familiarise and assess the multitude of various data and literature which formed the framework for the application. On studying the data over time it became more obvious to the reader that contradictions were in existence with one page expressing one point of view and another expressing the complete opposite. This reality once again highlighted the deficiencies involved in the application. I proceeded to make submissions highlighting my concerns and asked the planning section of Mayo County Council to refuse permission on the basis that this development did not comply with the sustainable development of the area. Submissions were also on file from the other statutory agencies involved in the planning process such as Dúchas (now the National Parks & Wildlife Service), the Health & Safety Authority, and the North Western Regional Fisheries Board.

Our concerns fell on deaf ears however as the important issues of concern were glossed over. Minister Frank Fahey wanted to be informed of the planning permission before it was formally announced as there was a letter to this effect on file from the Department. This issue was highlighted on a Channel 4 news item whereby Frank Fahey denied that he had interfered in the planning process. On a Friday afternoon and a bank holiday weekend dated August 3, 2001, at 4.55pm Mayo County Council announced that they had granted permission to the developer with 66 conditions attached. This was subsequently announced on MidWest radio on the five o'clock news bulletin.

Needless to say the next step involved finding out how an appeal would be made to An Bord Pleanála as there was a period of one month allocated before the deadline from the time the decision was granted so time was of the essence. I had to familiarise myself with finding out so much information in such a short time period and this was very difficult and challenging for me as I was more accustomed to working on the family farm as opposed to lodging appeals to various agencies. As a result of the information which I had read and in conjunction with other residents an appeal was lodged as it was our view that Mayo County Council were not in the possession of all of the facts involved in an application of this magnitude and thus should not have granted permission. This extra workload and the introduction of so much paperwork into the family home also created concern for my wife Aggie who was worried that the workload involved would become a burden as time went on. We were also very concerned about the proposed pipeline system as it had been excluded from the planning process apart from a tiny section contained within the refinery footprint. No statutory agency appeared to be taking responsibility for it regarding health and safety and environmental issues so it appeared to us as if we were in a state of limbo.

This reality added more fuel to the fire and we felt very vulnerable and alone in our dilemma with nobody to turn to for assistance. Sadly it appeared that this was going to be an uphill battle with the local residents engaging in the seeking out of knowledge and forming links with other environmental groups in seeking and highlighting facts based on common sense. This reality imposed a great burden on people who had limited resources compared to the oil consortium and the State. It represented a perfect example of David and Goliath and was highly exhaustive at times but also hugely rewarding as new friends and contacts were established thus removing somewhat the feeling of isolation which we felt. International links were formed with the Ogoni people in Nigeria, whose environment had been destroyed by Shell, who had oil and gas industrial operations there, and the Ecumenical Council for Corporate Responsibility (ECCR) who were based in the United Kingdom.

After appeals were lodged with An Bord Pleanála, the board decided to hold two oral hearings in February and November of 2002 respectively. The overall hearing in its combined form was to become the 2nd longest hearing in the history of the State which once again was reflective of the complexity of the issues involved. They were held in Ballina and this meant that we had to travel a daily round trip of 80 miles plus to attend whereas representatives of Enterprise Energy Ireland actually stayed in the hotel and had all their equipment set up in rooms in the vicinity of the hearing hall. Once again this demonstrated how local people were placed at a disadvantage in the process as they did not have their equipment and paper records at their disposal for reference. The Senior Inspector assigned to the appeal was Kevin Moore and he was accompanied by David Ball (a consultant hydrologist). When the first oral hearing was held in February Brian Ó Catháin was the Managing Director of EEI and was present at the hearing and was cross-examined. He was a native of Belfast and was a fluent Irish speaker. This tactic seemed to be a ploy at the time to blend in with the natives as they resided in a Gaeltacht area. This was however as far as conversing in the Irish language went as we were informed that English was the preferred language.

In April of 2002 it was announced that the Royal Dutch Shell consortium had acquired Enterprise Oil. Thus Shell took over the development concept as the main operator with the largest shareholding. As a consequence of this development Andy Pyle became the new Managing Director of EEI and was also present at the second oral hearing held in November of 2002. The two inspectors' approach with respect to all parties was meticulous in dealing with the complexities involved in the analysis of the overall application, the largest in the history of County Mayo and indeed the State. In his final report to the Board which was highly comprehensive in detail, Mr Moore stated among other things that the development as proposed was on the wrong site. The following extract is quoted from his report:

'From a strategic planning perspective this is the wrong site. From the perspective of government policy which seeks to foster regional development, this is the wrong site; from the perspective of minimising environmental impact, this is the wrong site; and consequently, from the perspective of sustainable development, this is the wrong site.'

Mr Moore also addressed the Off-Shore development option as Shell as operators had claimed that it was too expensive. This was in 2003 and beggared belief considering the multinational had declared QUARTERLY PROFITS OF ALMOST $4 BILLION. There were three offshore options available apart from the unprecedented option presently under scrutiny.

THE OPTIONS

- A deepwater fixed steel jacket;
- A shallow water (<100m depth) fixed steel jacket;
- A Tension Leg Platform (TLP), a buoyant SPAR platform, deep raft semi-submersible floating platform, or tanker-based floating production vessel.

The Board of An Bord Pleanála in their analysis of the overall findings derived from the report stated: 'Finally the Board noted that alternatives are available for the development of the Corrib Gas field.' This was substantiated by the Inspector under the heading (2.0) Alternatives, where the Board were dissatisfied with the information provided by the developers despite being specifically requested to address an alternative option. No feasibility assessments had or have been conducted to date despite the reality that offshore technology has been available for years i.e. in the North Sea which recovers and processes oil and gas at source. The North Sea is located further north than the Atlantic and thus harsher sea conditions are experienced and offshore equipment utilised can also extract hydrocarbons at much greater depths than experienced at the Corrib field. In my opinion it is a very ironic reflection that this technology is utilised by Statoil who in turn have a 36.5% shareholding in this venture, and yet proceed to hide behind Shell as operator to deliver this inadequate project. It would appear that they uphold the best standards in their own territory fully intent on seeking out better technologies and yet deviate from these set standards when it comes to doing it on the cheap elsewhere.

The Board refused planning permission on the basis that the transfer and removal of 650,000 cubic metres of peat to adjoining land on the site would constitute an environmental risk to local waterways. On a Prime Time programme shortly aired after this decision was made, Minister Frank Fahey projected that Shell Exploration & Production Ireland Limited (who had replaced Enterprise Energy Ireland Limited) should reapply and submit a new application which would deal with the peat issue. He was of the view that this was the only problem which stood in their way which of course was not the true reflection as serious environmental and safety issues were at stake.

LANDSLIDES

On September 19, 2003 the Taoiseach Bertie Ahern met with senior Shell executives. These included Andy Pyle (Managing Director of SEPIL), and Tom Botts (Chief Executive Officer of Shell Exploration & Production Europe). The Taoiseach was accompanied by Minister Dermot Ahern, who had taken over the role of the Department of Communications, Marine & Natural Resources, and the Minister for the Environment, Martin Cullen. The Shell executives told the Taoiseach that they would like 'a greater dialogue with the planning authorities, especially ABP (An Bord Pleanála)'. Mr Ahern assured them that the government would seek to facilitate the project but it would have to go through the planning process. On the night of the 19th September 2003 a multitude of over 44 simultaneous landslides created a combined avalanche of mud, gravel, peat and various debris including concrete walls, swept bridges, fencing, swept animals etc. all of which meandered down the Glengad, Barnacuille, and Cornhill mountains. This debris swept through homes and removed sacred graves in the local cemetery which were washed into the sea. It was extremely fortunate that nobody was killed, and local people were in complete shock as the reality of the events which had occurred unfolded before their eyes. The events represented a scene from a horror film. The debris also displaced local waterways which in effect meant that the displaced water led to extensive flooding elsewhere. The Ballinaboy River was flooded which drained the site at Ballinaboy. The debris also ran downhill towards the shoreline which was where the proposed landfall was located. If the original Pullathomas route had been implemented at that stage it would have been unearthed and a major catastrophic accident would have been unavoidable. As tonnes of debris were deposited on the shoreline this also resulted in a boreen leading to the shore being severely cratered. This material would also have impacted on the revised route if it was in place as its location was also directly beneath the mountain and thus if highly volatile and pressured gas had been flowing, which included a valve station at the landfall, lives would almost certainly have been lost. In a recent survey conducted by the GSI, it was reported that landslides similar to what occurred will be more frequent in future.

It was the concerned residents in the area who had delayed the laying of the pipeline complex, not Shell and the State agencies. It had been pointed out at the oral hearing with respect to the terminal/refinery application by residents that landslides were quiet common in the area. Mr John Colreavy of the Health & Safety Authority had stated that the authority had not taken landslides into account in their assessment regarding a gas explosion event on/or off site. This was damning in light of what had just occurred. To add insult to injury Shell proceeded with their plans for the area and submitted a revised application to Mayo County Council as if this event had not taken place. This in my opinion again was highly reflective of the contempt and utter arrogance which they displayed towards the people in our area. It was a complete abomination. When the Taoiseach was later questioned in the Dail about the meeting which was held with the Shell executives, among other matters, he stated that, 'At the moment we are at the end of a pipeline that gives us access to almost unlimited amounts of gas from Russia. Those who know more about this than I do can see the potential down the road. If this resource works effectively, as some of the early studies suggest, we could be exporting gas to the UK.' He seemed to forget the events of 1992 and how the Irish State had been sold out by Fianna Fáil, and its resources given away, and thus the Irish people had no longer any say in the matter.

Shell Exploration and Production Ireland Limited (SEPIL) submitted a new application P03/3343 on the 17th December 2003 to Mayo County Council. This time the application included the proposal to remove the liquid peat offsite to an area of cut-away peatland in Srahmore, near Bangor Erris. It was intended that Bord Na Mona would carry out this work on behalf of Shell. A waste licence was also applied for to the Environmental Protection Agency to remove the peat off-site. There was also a proposal to use highly alkaline cement binder to strengthen peat in certain areas of the site. The proposal re Srahmore in effect extended the pollution risks to the wider Erris area as more waterways surrounding the site re drainage patterns in Srahmore were to be implicated. These included the Munhin and Owenmore rivers which drained into Tullaghan Bay in Geesala. Needless to say the monster as I saw it and its waste products were now to be spread rapidly over the Erris area.

On the 30th of April 2004 Mayo County Council granted permission to the developers. This was once again appealed by concerned residents in the area to An Bord Pleanála. An oral hearing was requested and refused. On the 22nd of October 2004 the deputy planning officer assigned to the application Des R Johnson recommended that the application should get the go-ahead. This decision was unanimously backed up by the Board.

In Mr Johnson's report he did state the following however: 'I am concerned that, in the event of excess solids being discharged to the Bellanaboy River, Carrowmore Lake could effectively become a giant settlement pond. It is critical that this does not occur as deposition of peat particles on the floor of the lake would have a seriously detrimental impact and would be difficult, if not impossible, to remove.'

The EPA also granted the waste licence for the removal of the peat to Srahmore. This was predicted under the circumstances. It was stated in the Western People newspaper dated December 15, 2004, that Andy Pyle had addressed a media briefing in Breaffy House Hotel and that it was a case of all systems go. He also stated that gas would flow from the Ballinaboy terminal into the national grid by the year 2007. The earthworks contract was awarded to Roadbridge Limited, and Mayo County Council began preparatory works to improve the R311 road for the removal and transfer of the liquid peat which was to be transported a distance of 11km away. In April of 2005 peat haulage operations had to be suspended practically before they began as a series of road incidents occurred. A number of haulage trucks carrying the liquid peat ran into difficulties and overturned off the road into the bog. This posed a serious danger to other road users as these trucks were to conduct 800 return journeys per day from Ballinaboy to Srahmore. The whole sorry saga had begun.

COMPULSORY ACQUISITION ORDERS

As local landowners objected to the placing of this unprecedented pipeline complex on their lands this resulted in the Minister for the Marine & Natural Resources Frank Fahey purportedly making Compulsory Acquisition Orders (CAO) for the lands in question. On November 15, 2001 the Minister introduced SI 517 of 2001 which purported to amend the Gas Act of 1976 so that he could grant the order to the developers. This process meant in effect that a private company could acquire private land and do with it as they pleased. On November 23, 2001 Ronan Daly & Jermyn Solicitors informed me that unless I signed up and gave into their demands, that they reserved the right to commence CAO procedures. I did not sign the necessary paperwork. A notice of application for acquisition orders under Section 32 of the Gas Act 1976 was published in the Western People newspaper. A notice of entry was also produced in May 2002. At this stage the matter had been amended by the Gas (Interim)(Regulation) Act 2002 and SI 517 was revoked. Myself and my neighbours as residents living along and in close proximity to this development were to be subjected to unquantified risks not normally associated with compulsory acquisition. It was my belief that the Irish Constitution was to protect the citizens of this State from unjust laws which did not reconcile with this proposal as outlined.

On January 10/11, 2005 representatives of EEI attempted to gain entry onto certain lands in Rossport. On January 11 they returned to once again attempt entry. This occurred in gale force storms of over 93 miles per hour, and the employees of SEPIL and local people were in danger of getting injured. The events which unfolded were witnessed by Mr Denny Larson who was affiliated to the Global Community Monitor Environmental Organisation (GCMEO). He expressed shock at what he had witnessed as schools and other public buildings were closed due to the weather and yet employees were out in such winds with their hard safety hats falling off in the prevailing storm. He expressed this view on the MidWest local radio news bulletin which was aired that evening.

At the end of February representatives of SEPIL once again attempted to gain entry onto the lands. They were refused by all the landowners who had not consented to the CAO's on the basis that they had not released the relevant paperwork which demonstrated that they had the authority to do what they proposed. They explained that their paperwork was in order, but that we would not be allowed to view it. The landowners in question received a summons which was stamped March 4, and it stated that legal Counsel appearing on behalf of SEPIL would apply to the High Court on March 14, 2005 for an interlocutory injunction restraining the named defendants from interfering with their entry on to the lands in question. At this stage I realised that events were getting very serious indeed.

THE COURTS

On March 14, 2005 myself, and Bríd Mc Garry who was also a listed defendant, presented ourselves in the High Court. We had decided to represent ourselves and conduct our own defences because we felt that we had an in-depth knowledge of the details involved. From my own point of view I felt there was something wrong when I had requested documents from the Department of Marine, documents that they had in their possession and which they refused to make available to me. The other defendants i.e. Philip McGrath, Willie Corduff, Monica Muller, and Peter Sweetman were represented by Legal Counsel. The hearing was conducted over a period of four days and was heard before the President of the High Court, Justice Joseph Finnegan. On the fourth day of the hearing Justice Finnegan granted an interlocutory injunction to the plaintiff. We were overwhelmed by this judgement as this meant that SEPIL would be allowed to construct and lay the pipeline complex on our lands. Justice Finnegan did state however that the gas would not be allowed to flow until a full hearing with respect to the issues involved was determined.

On June 13, 2005 Mark Carrigy (Operations Manager for proposed refinery) notified me (and the defendants individually) via telephone that he wished to arrange a meeting with respect to entry and that SEPIL would attempt to gain entry at the "latter end of the week". He indicated that a meeting was set up for Friday. I indicated that I would revert back to him with respect to his request. On June 15, which was on a Wednesday, Andy Pyle (Managing Director of SEPIL) conducted an extensive public relations interview on the Tommy Marron morning show on MidWest local radio. During the 30-minute interview he projected a totally biased and self-serving account of all aspects of their pipeline/refinery activities. It was acknowledged later that he had stipulated that no calls were to be taken during his interview despite this being the norm for this very popular chat show.

By mid afternoon I was in the middle of preparing a fax stating that we would meet with Mark Carrigy on Friday when I received an anxious call telling me that SEPIL representatives were attempting to gain access to lands in Rossport. They were accompanied by the Gardaí who proceeded to take names and addresses of the individuals who had denied entry. After they were refused access by the relevant landowners there, they drove over to the village of Gortacragher where Bríd and Teresa Mc Garry lived and attempted to gain entry there. Bríd informed them in Irish that she wished to see the official papers, na páipéirí oifigiúla, that they were relying on. These papers were not produced so she refused entry on that basis. Bríd was aware that SEPIL had breached the Ministers order (that phase of the Minister's consent was not granted to them) as she had observed works which had taken place in the Coillte property across from her residence. The developers were only allowed at that stage to survey, set-out and fence off. They had actually conducted extensive works however including the placing of sheet piles into the bedrock and had also welded pipes together which went beyond their remit. On the 16th of June SEPIL employees attempted to gain entry onto my lands in Rossport South. I also refused entry and spoke to them in Irish as we live in a Gaeltacht area. I also informed them that I wished to see the official papers, "na páipéirí oifigiúla", that they were relying on. These papers were not produced so I also refused entry on that basis.

SEPIL applied to the High Court to commence attachment and committal proceedings.

IMPRISONMENT

We attended in the High Court on June 29, 2005. We had left Rossport at 4.30am that morning. I attempted to explain to the Court the reasons why I felt I could not give an undertaking to comply with the Court Order. I was dumbfounded by what was happening before my eyes. The following is an extract of events published in the Irish Times newspaper, dated June 30, 2005: 'James Philbin said the court had only heard from Shell a "one-sided version" of events and "a lot of untruths". He had reason to believe a quantifiable risk assessment on the pipeline had not been independently carried out, but despite this a multinational oil company had been given the right to build the pipeline in front of his and other houses for their own gain. He believed there was no valid ministerial consent for this development. He also said a road servicing the development was inadequate and denied he had blocked that road. Ireland would not gain one cent from this development and Shell was seeking to "make criminals out of us".'

The Legal Counsel representing SEPIL succeeded in their application for our committal to prison. They also sought and secured costs for the application. We were imprisoned before a full hearing had taken place on the substantive issues which were involved in this case. I felt totally dejected as I had done everything in my power to prevent our community from being placed at unprecedented risk and had treated SEPIL and the State agencies with the utmost respect at all times. Now I was going to have to pay a very personal price as well.

I looked around the courtroom at the other men and their wives, the look of total shock etched on their faces. Nobody could believe what was happening. Bríd Mc Garry who sat beside me during the hearing as we were still presenting ourselves, was speechless and in total shock. All this happened so fast that the next thing we knew Court Gardai were leading us away to the Bridewell Garda Station across the street. We were surrounded by people and I remember Joe Higgins (Socialist TD) was there, Michael Ring (Fine Gael TD) who had supported our cause from inception, and Dr. Jerry Cowley (Independent TD) were also present as well as a good number of our loyal supporters who had also travelled from home that morning. There was a media frenzy outside the Bridewell and interviews were given highlighting the injustice which had occurred in north Mayo. After information was recorded in the Garda Station we were transferred to Mountjoy prison that evening. A protest had gathered outside the gates of the jail and this lifted our spirits somewhat. The Gardai were highly courteous and affable to us at all times and this made us feel a bit more at ease. That evening we were once again transferred to the Cloverhill remand prison, which was where we remained for the 94 days of our detention.

We were kept informed of local events which were occurring in Bellanaboy and Rossport by Dr. Jerry Cowley (Independent TD). He and Dr. Mark Garavan visited us on a regular basis in Cloverhill prison over the 94-day period. Events were also highlighted in the local and national media and it was reassuring to know that at last our side of the story was going to reach the wider public arena after years of trying to get the truth into the wider public domain. We were informed that mass demonstrations were occurring at Ballinaboy and at the Rossport compound on a daily basis. A well informed group of individuals and activists from all over the country and who later went on to form the Rossport Solidarity Camp were highly supportive and great credit is due to their efforts in highlighting the cause.

We received great support from our fellow prisoners and prison wardens in Cloverhill and tried to become accustomed to prison life. We had to wear prison clothes and were locked in our cells after eight o'clock in the evening. Myself, and Philip and Willie were in one cell, and Mícheál and Vincent were in the other. After a while we began to feel as if we were being institutionalised as our prison door was opened and closed before us, and there was a set pattern re routine. We had to go to the end of the corridor to collect our breakfast, main dinner and tea at the same time each day, and we also were given a set time for exercise in the yards. This was difficult to adjust to as I was so used to having no set routine as I worked the family farm, and also loved the outdoor life so being locked up for most of the day and my freedom taken away was most difficult to come to terms with.

The first few days were most difficult for everyone. For my wife Aggie and my family it was extremely difficult as they had to face challenging times. It was the first time since our marriage that myself and Aggie were separated from each other. SEPIL had done this to us, what else were they capable of at this stage? The family had to be very tough and courageous as they familiarised themselves and became accustomed to dealing with visiting the prison. They did not know what to expect. They had to travel up from our home in Rossport which meant that they had to leave in the early hours to ensure they arrived in time for the prison hours as visits were limited to one a day, and there were time restrictions also imposed. On entering the prison the family were met by a series of security gates and locks which from a psychological viewpoint was very difficult for them to take in. After going through the administration process they were finally met with a glass screen where we were allowed to converse and no physical contact was allowed. Once again this was very difficult for them and for me to deal with. I valued greatly the time we spent together and it was very difficult when they were asked to leave as the time we had together passed by so quickly. Their visits kept me informed and uplifted and I also looked forward to visits from my siblings who regularly called in to see me.

My family kept me well informed of events and I greatly admired how they rose to the challenge by contributing to local and national rallies and thus speaking to the thousands of people who supported the campaign for SHELL TO SEA. They also had to deal with the huge media interest (local, national, and international) and conduct extensive interviews. This aspect was very demanding and challenging as their lives were not their own as they were catapulted into the public arena. The family knew that the cause was just and were aware of this ongoing saga regarding the pipeline and the refinery. They also had to strive to strike a balance and keep the family day-to-day running of the household running smoothly. It was great to see our extended family rally around and offer any help they could, with respect to the different tasks that needed to be done on the farm over the summer months. In September Aggie tried to keep events as normal as possible as two of our daughters had to prepare to return to college in Dublin. Our youngest daughter also had to return to secondary school to begin her Leaving Certificate final year.

While the family were kept busy at home, I was kept busy reading letters, cards, and postcards of support which I received in their hundreds from people in Ireland, and all over the world offering solidarity and encouraging words. I was overwhelmed that people would take the time to write to me and the other men and this was greatly encouraging. It was great to see so many of the artistic slogans at home being printed in the national papers. At this stage I had also decided to work in the prison kitchen as this helped to pass the time. The kitchen staff were most courteous to me and I was very grateful that I was allowed to pass away the hours there.

On September 19 a delegation which included my son Chris, Dr. Jerry Cowley (TD), Anthony Irwin, Caitlín Uí Seighin, and John Monaghan left to visit Norway to visit members of the new labour government and representatives of Statoil. The function for the delegation was to highlight Norway's role in the impasse as Statoil was 71% Norwegian State-owned, and they in turn held a 36.5% share in the Corrib gas field. The visit was a major success. Up to this point SEPIL had stated that they could not collapse the injunction and that they would continue to look for a mechanism to resolve the situation. On the 2nd of October it was reported in the Sunday Business Post that, 'A senior Statoil executive travelled to Dublin last week and is believed to have played a key role. Helga Hattlested, executive vice chairman of Statoil, met representatives of Shell – the largest shareholder in the Corrib field – and the Department of Marine, Communications and Natural Resources, under Minister Noel Dempsey ...' This recent development certainly was no coincidence.

Towards the end of September, over 40 academics in University College Dublin issued a letter which declared that the imprisonment of the Rossport 5 was an 'affront to the conscience of Irish society ...' The letter also stated that the Corrib Gas Consortium had used the courts to jail the five men and that those same companies had acted outside of the law by laying a pipeline without ministerial consent. It also stated that Shell had yet to advance a convincing argument as to why Corrib gas could not be processed at sea.

RELEASE

On September 30, 2005, which was on a Friday, we were released from Cloverhill prison. It was wonderful to be finally reunited with my family and friends. We received a very warm reception from everyone and it was wonderful to be on free soil once more. We appeared on the Late Late Show that night and I tried to thank as many people as I could as they were all amazing in my eyes. We also participated in the rally in Dublin the next day which was very well attended. We also had to conduct many media interviews. This gave me an insight into what my family had to cope with over the summer months. The return journey home to Mayo was electrifying with bonfires lit on route. We met many well-wishers, and people who welcomed us home. After the first few days it was back to the old routine of talking about the gas, Shell, and the pipeline. That was the main topic of the day. After coming out of prison you could see it in the wider community that what Shell had done by imprisoning the five of us was really the last straw, and personally speaking I can categorically see that the people see Shell in a different light, regardless of their PR exercises. The legal case into the substantive issues is still pending.

Thus this sorry saga is far from over for the people of this community.

CHAPTER 5

'We were not overawed, we had right on our side'

Vincent and Maureen McGrath

VINCENT My ancestors have lived here in Rossport for many generations, at least six generations, in the same spot along the shore on the northern side of Sruth Fada Conn, that is the estuary of the Glenamoy River that flows into Broadhaven Bay. The home place down by the shore is called Rinn na Rón, where the seals used to congregate and sometimes come ashore. That's where I was born and reared. So we've been here a long time and as you'd expect we have a strong attachment to the land and a deep sense of belonging to the place has been built up over many generations. The McGraths first came into this area from the southeast Donegal–northwest Fermanagh region of Ulster. Indeed most families around here have their origins in the north of Ireland and are descendants of people who were forced to leave their homes in Ulster because of the Transplantation of Cromwell in 1650. That's when they were given the choice of To Hell or to Connaught.

The farms are small around here but still the people have managed to eke out a living by growing their own potatoes and vegetables. They would also supplement their income by selling a few sheep or cattle. The bog has always been an integral part of the lives of the people and our knowledge and understanding of the bog has proven to be invaluable in our present struggle. As well as fuelling the fires people also made a few pounds by selling turf. There was a tradition of that type of farming – 'subsistence' farming, or 'peasant' farming I think that's called, that way of life, going back unchanged perhaps for a couple of hundred years. That old way of life stayed on here for a long time and I'm glad to have seen it and to be part of it.

We didn't have a tradition of secondary education here. It was normal for boys and girls to go to England after they had finished primary school and sometimes they didn't even wait to finish. There was a secondary school in Belmullet but it was a boarding school for girls. Only those who were well off could afford to send their daughters there. We were no better off than everybody else but my father worked very hard and managed to send my older sister to the convent in Belmullet. He believed in education and believed that it would give us the kind of opportunities in life that he had missed out on. He often told us that in the course of his travels in England and America he had got many good job offers and opportunities but he didn't have the confidence to accept them because of what he perceived to be his lack of education. I suppose what he was really saying is that information and knowledge empowers you and gives you confidence and that's another thing we've learned here in Rossport from this campaign.

Then in 1959 Gael Linn, a body set up to promote the Irish language, opened a secondary school here in Rossport called Coláiste Chomáin. For those of us who were going to the National school at the time that was the worst thing that could have happened to us or so we felt at the time. It meant that now we'd have to go to the Coláiste and miss out on the opportunity to see the world or some of it at least. We'd been looking forward to going off to England at fourteen or fifteen years of age. Instead of that we were now being 'forced', as we saw it, to stay on at school. I went to Coláiste Chomáin in 1962. That coincided with Micheál Ó Seighin's arrival as a teacher in Rossport. He came to school to teach the day I started at secondary school.

After completing the Leaving Certificate I didn't go straight on to Third Level but instead went off to England where I worked for a while in Reading and I lived and worked for about a year in

Cambridge. Would you believe that I worked for a while on the North Sea gas pipeline with the subcontractors Press and Chambers? As far as I remember John Browne was the main contractor – CJB, I think. Pipeline diameter didn't concern us too much at the time and the bars we talked about had nothing to do with high pressure. I worked for about ten months with a civil engineering contractor by the name of Jackson. Basically that involved providing basic infrastructure like roads and sewers before a housing estate was built. My main job was mixing concrete. I loved the physical work and still do.

There were two brothers of the Jacksons, Alan and Basil. They were from Northern Ireland and their foreman was Tom Keaveney from Galway. I don't know what part of Northern Ireland they were from but I remember on the 12th July that Basil put an orange leaf (or the nearest colour he could find) on the dumper he was driving around the site. I was told that he did that every year when he couldn't be at home for the occasion. He often told me that when he was young his neighbours would look down on them because they were poor. So poverty and snobbery have no religious bounds.

I didn't intend to return to Ireland at that stage of my life but I did come home for Christmas and the teachers in Coláiste Chomáin gave me a teaching job although I wasn't fully qualified. I suppose they thought I was wasting my time over in England. After a year and a half teaching I went to University College, Galway.

It was very unusual at that time for somebody from around here to go to university. I don't think that we could have afforded it if I hadn't got a Gaeltacht Scholarship. Cars were not as affordable in those days and it wasn't practical for me to come home every weekend and I would only come home at mid-term breaks and during the holidays. I always wanted to teach. It was my vocation at that time. I studied Irish, History and Geography - and Economics for one year. All my lectures were through Irish.

I lived for twenty-five years in County Louth on the East Coast of Ireland. I went to work in the community school in Ardee in 1974 as a teacher of Irish and later I also taught History and Geography. As well as living in Ardee I lived in the town of Dunleer but for most of the time I lived in Drogheda. I retired early from teaching and I returned home to live in Rossport with my wife, Maureen, and two girls, Máire and Deirdre. We built this house in 1997. That coincided with the start of the gas and talk about the gas coming ashore. Good timing!

MAUREEN I'm from Aghoose, which is just across the estuary here. I went to school in Belmullet. I joined the Civil Service and worked in quite a number of places – Carrick on Shannon at first, Lifford for a few years, Ballybofey and Ballina. I also worked in Sheriff Street in Dublin for a while. After we got married we lived in Drogheda.

VINCENT We were married here in the local Parish Church, Aghoose in 1982. Our two girls were born in Drogheda. Máire was christened here and Deirdre was christened in Drogheda. They both went to Fatima School before we came down here. As I said, we came back down here about ten years ago.

MAUREEN Drogheda was getting very much like Dublin. It had changed a lot.

VINCENT I suppose the savage loves his native shore. There's that in all of us. Especially when you have children you ask yourself where is the best place to bring them up. A parent always thinks about safety. The main thing is the quality of life. You want them to have some of the childhood experiences you had yourself like the freedom to wander the open countryside. Before the children go to secondary school is a good time to make that move. I'm glad my girls were young enough to have experienced some of that freedom by coming back here.

Between Maureen and me we have extensive networks and ties in the area. There are twelve in my family – nine boys and three girls. My oldest brother died when he was about two years old so we don't remember him. That would leave thirteen or the baker's dozen. I'm in the middle – six older, six younger. My father used to say jokingly that he would need to take a roll call at mealtimes to make sure that we were all present. But ten or twelve was a typical size family at the time. I remember gangs of us used to play football out in the fields, even in the moonlight. Parents didn't have the worries of modern life. We looked after each other. We didn't have the choices of today so we weren't spoiled for choice. What we didn't have we didn't miss. That was our little World. It may have been a small World but I can honestly say it was a very happy one.

Except, of course, we knew about England. We envied those who went to England in a way. When they came home they were always well dressed. They seemed to look better than when they had left. They would look healthier. There was a bit of opulence about them. Perhaps they had saved up and made an effort to show off when they came home at Christmas and for the summer. It was our ambition to join them in England. No one seemed to have any interest in staying on the farm. It was a way of life that many people wanted to discard, not just the poverty and the rural way of life but the language and the music and anything associated with it. Of course, there was a lot of repression in the way people lived and behaved. The Church was a very strong force in people's lives. There was a certain overpowering atmosphere around. People talked about people. We didn't have the freedom that young people need, the freedom to be anonymous, to get on with their life, to act as teenagers, to be wild. I remember being in London for the first time and feeling a great sense of freedom to do what I liked without some-body looking over my shoulder. On the other hand a lot of the people here were more broadminded than most. Our fathers and most of the older people we knew had been to England so they had travelled a lot. But the thing is we wanted to go away. Today too, young people want to get away from the countryside and be where the action is.

MAUREEN My family wasn't really like that. For us going to England wasn't that big. I think, maybe the nuns had a lot to do with that. They used to say to us as a threat 'You'll end up over there' – whatever that meant! The nuns were very nationalistic, very much into language and history. Civics was a big thing for them. Actually most of my class settled down here. They didn't go away.

There was little Irish spoken in Aghoose. My father had a bit of Irish but there was never Irish spoken at home. Next door they had Irish.

VINCENT Funny enough, it often depends on who speaks first. Even today when you meet someone it depends on who speaks first and whether it's in Irish or English. People can easily switch from one to the other.

For us at home and in Rossport there was a lot of Irish, although English had taken over as the main language. I was lucky to have spent a lot of time with my grandmother. She preferred to speak Irish. She was a very intelligent woman and was a great source of music and folklore. I got a lot of that from her. I was very influenced by her. As a teenager I used to spend hours sitting down by the turf fire in her room writing down a lot of her folklore and stories. I suppose that was a bit unusual for a teenager. I'd say it was because of her that music is so much part of my life and that I am so aware of my own tradition and my musical tradition in particular. The same goes for the language.

WHEN WAS THE FIRST WORD ABOUT THE GAS PROJECT?

MAUREEN We didn't know about the gas when we came back. We got planning permission for this house in 1996 or 1997. The gas hadn't come up then. We were already in this house before it really started off.

VINCENT It started off about 2000. At the beginning I wasn't involved.

MAUREEN Our daughter Deirdre was still in National school at the time. The first we really heard about the gas was when there was a petition in support of it in the Western People. Deirdre came home from school saying how it was a great thing and she was signing it of course. Most of the people thought at the time that it was great.

VINCENT I think the position was when the gas was discovered that there was a campaign to bring it into Mayo. Local people thought it would be something like Kinsale. They can be forgiven for thinking that because if you look back at the glossy brochures they gave out at the time there is no hint that what they were proposing here was any different. That was as much as people knew. There was a lot of talk and hype about the great benefits it would bring. We were so lucky. It was Mayo gas. The farmers whose land the pipeline would run through would make a lot of money. They were the lucky ones. I think they were envied a little at the time. People were pointing to Aberdeen, to places where oil was brought ashore and they were saying that it would bring a lot of wealth and prosperity. Words like windfall and bonanza were used but words such as health, safety and danger didn't enter into the discourse in the beginning. It wouldn't have been very popular to do so. That was basically it at the time.

MAUREEN It was all very vague at the beginning. It had just been found and it could have been processed anywhere along the West Coast. The thing was at the time to have it done in Mayo.

VINCENT I don't know when information first came out about the actual nature of the gas and the refinery. We weren't involved early on. I think our neighbours, the Mullers, were the first to raise concerns. They went to Micheál Ó Seighin to get him involved. They were very nervous about it and felt that there was something seriously wrong with the project. They saw that the plans were for something very substantial, quite different from Kinsale. Ballinaboy had been chosen at this stage as the site for processing the gas.

At first the pipeline was to come in through Pollathomas across the estuary from Rossport. Later on, I think it was in 2001 my nephew Alan asked me if I had heard that the pipeline was coming through Rossport. However, for personal reasons I hadn't come on board the campaign at that stage. I was aware of the meetings that were going on, the so-called 'consultations'. I went to a public meeting in Rossport some time later to see what was happening. It was being held to elect a local representative on to the Environmental Monitoring Group. Michael Daly, Principal Officer of the Petroleum Affairs Division in the Department of Marine and Natural Resources was there along with the Assistant Principal Officer, Carmel Murray. She only wanted somebody from Rossport on the EMG and Michael Daly said that anybody who was objecting to the project would not be a 'suitable' person to serve on the EMG. The people of Ballinaboy walked out of the meeting in disgust. Some of us from Rossport walked out along with them. This wasn't planned. It was a spontaneous reaction to the charade we had just witnessed. That was the first meeting I had attended and it was obvious that the Department only wanted 'yes men' to enable the project to go ahead without any hassle. That has been the pattern ever since. I remember feeling a sense of unease at the lack of openness and the suppression of legitimate discussion and I started to think seriously about the whole project and what it was about this project that they were afraid to discuss openly. I sent an email to the then Minister for Communications, Marine and Natural Resources, Dermot Aherne, complaining about the conduct of the Rossport meeting. I remember comparing what happened to the Nice Treaty that had been put to the people a second time because the Government didn't get the 'right' result the first time. They had ignored the wishes of the people and this was also happening in Rossport. I sent the email to the Petroleum Affairs Division but with hindsight I'd say the Minister probably never received it, not that it would have mattered even if he had.

Because the pipeline wasn't going through our land Enterprise Energy Ireland (they sold to Shell in 2002) didn't require our consent. They had been speaking to other landowners but they hadn't come near us. It angered me though because we learned later how dangerous the gas was and here we were the closest to the pipeline route and yet we were being completely ignored. As far as they were concerned we didn't matter. That still seems to be their position today. In their public pronouncements they talk about engaging with the local community and consulting with stakeholders but if they don't have to deal with you they just ignore you. A stakeholder is somebody affected by a project but the company's definition appears to be somebody who helps them to get the project through. At least that's how they have acted. But here we were, the local residents, closest to the pipeline, the people who would be in most danger if an accident happened and yet they ignored us. The only information we ever got directly was in February 2005 when they were about to start laying the pipeline in front of our house. They informed us then by letter about the noise levels we would experience. That was it. Fait accompli. If you don't wish, they said, there will be no work on Sunday. Alleluia!

MAUREEN We were never consulted about the route. There was not a word. It was as if we didn't exist. On one occasion their local rep visited the house but I realised later that it was probably to see how near we were to the route. I remember during the 2002 election Fianna Fáil canvassers called and remarked on how we had a lovely view. I said to them what about that terminal. They said, 'oh, we won't talk about that.' They said that it would be coming in anyway.

VINCENT That was the whole approach – a fait accompli. It's coming in anyway. Everything they did came from this idea they had planted in the public mind. Even Frank Fahey, the Minister for Marine and Natural Resources and the man who gave the go-ahead to the Plan of Development, said in the Dáil that the people of Erris were entitled to object but they couldn't hold up the project. That was the message that was going out, the psychological message. We'll take on board your concerns but the project is going ahead as planned. You cannot do anything about it. It's too important. The interests pushing it are too powerful. You're only a little guy. That's it.

Then I read the Environmental Impact Statement for myself. I concentrated particularly on the 9km onshore section of the pipeline. I made copious notes on that. I could see all the contradictions and all the inadequacies. You could see that it was advocacy rather than objective analysis. You could see how they were trying to deceive by the way they used language. For example they said that the site they had chosen for the processing plant at Ballinaboy was not visible from the surrounding roads because of the trees. This was the sort of attempt they were making at trying to deceive us because while the site or the ground area might not be visible the 40 metres tall flare stacks would certainly be very visible. You could see how there was a lack of balance, how it was about pushing the project. The 'benefits' were highlighted and exaggerated while the potential dangers were described as 'unlikely'. My main concern was safety. I learned that this work was unprecedented, unique. I sent letters about the pipeline to the Minister. He assured me that it was safe, that I had nothing to worry about even in the event of a worst-case scenario. I knew this was untrue. The more I corresponded with the Department the more I realised that there were shared interests with the company, that there was collusion there. I had no doubt about that. They were singing in harmony.

We took them on, not in the violent manner they were hoping for, but we confronted them in a way they hadn't expected. A Nigerian visitor said to me that this was the first time that an oil company had been challenged on an intellectual level. We found that there were inconsistencies in their argument. They would tell us that some aspect was quite normal. So we'd look it up, we'd research it and we'd find that they were telling us lies. One night I had researched something about peat on the Internet that contradicted what they had said in the EIS and I brought it back to Micheál Ó Seighin. Micheál said, 'They won't con us.' Yet they were accusing us of putting out misinformation. We had several methods for extracting information. We'd write to relevant Departments, we'd do our own research, we'd get written answers to Dáil questions. We'd find out that they were withholding information. For example, they would not make public the original Quantified Risk Assessment on the pipeline. They still haven't. They were talking on the one hand about transparency and openness and consultation and yet when you wanted information they wouldn't divulge it. There was this inconsistency. We knew that they had a big, well-funded PR machine. We could only fight that by having the facts and by being upfront with the people and hoping they'd believe us.

What was worrying me most was the safety aspect. But, of course, we also found out in the course of our research about the 1992 Licensing Terms and the deal that was done between Ray Burke and the oil companies that gave away the people's natural resources of oil and gas for nothing. That only reinforced our resentment at what was going on. We'd get all the pain and the country would have no gain. It wouldn't have been too bad if the country as a whole had gained something. It seemed crazy that the people of Norway would own 25% of the gas because of Statoil's 36.5% stake in the Corrib Field and their 70% share in Statoil. And here we were being exposed to a high-risk, high-consequence project with little or no gain for Ireland. So it was the combination of a whole lot of factors that was motivating us, but safety was the main concern.

As well as that, it seemed to me that there was a derogation of our sovereignty to Shell. It was almost a Guantanamo Bay situation here. You'd have to be here when this was happening to see for yourself. There was a legal limbo here in Rossport and I believe that this was done on purpose. It was done to try and confuse us and make us feel helpless. They had Work in Progress and Sorry for the Inconvenience signs up all over the place but they never said who was carrying out the works, whether it was Mayo County Council or the contractors Roadbridge or Shell. And all the signs were in English even though this is a Gaeltacht or Irish-speaking area. Nobody seemed to be in charge and taking responsibility for our safety along the pipeline. The Department of the Marine and Natural Resources wouldn't take responsibility even though they had exempted the pipeline from planning permission. Mayo County Council's functional area went as far as the high-water mark but still they were not responsible for the 9km pipeline above the high-water mark. The Health and Safety Authority would take responsibility for the workers during the construction of the pipeline but they had no function when it came to the safety of residents of Rossport living along the pipeline. An Bord Pleanála had no function since the pipeline was exempted from planning permission. Our safety was being left in the hands of a private company whose track record around the world would not inspire confidence. When questioned about aspects of the project Statoil and Enterprise Energy Ireland (and their assigns Shell) would protest that they were only operating within the laws of this country. Of course they had lobbied politicians in the first place to change the law to facilitate the project. For example the 1976 Gas Act was amended specifically for the pipeline. When landowners would not consent to allowing the pipeline on their land Minister Frank Fahey brought in Compulsory Acquisition Orders. This was the first time that this was done for a private company and it has serious implications for private property rights in this country. It was brought in by the back door through a mechanism known as a Statutory Instrument and it was not even debated in the Dáil. I thought that the major farming organisations would be up in arms over this because of what it could mean for their members but so far there has been only silence. Malcolm Thompson of the ICSA (Irish Cattle and Sheep Association) is an exception.

MAUREEN You didn't expect that to happen but you weren't shocked either when it did happen in our case.

VINCENT We weren't surprised because we knew there was a democratic deficit in the country. They weren't going to listen to ordinary people. They weren't used to doing that. For example, the planning system is designed in such a way that you can go right through the whole process and let off some steam but in the end the major projects get their way. They can just say that a particular development is in accordance with Government policy or that it's in the National Interest. So what's the point of all this planning process when you're going to lose anyway? Safety doesn't come into it, only planning matters are taken into account. Safety should be at the top of the pyramid but it's way down. The plan is approved and the EPA grants a licence afterwards. And of course they tell us that there will be strict monitoring of the project, as if monitoring is prevention. The result is that projects are approved and if and when the developers transgress they are fined a derisory sum and they carry on as before. I believe that large companies like Shell monitor themselves. If I believed that the monitoring bodies in this country were able and willing to do their job then there would be no need for the likes of me to get involved to the extent I did. I'd be happy to leave my safety in their hands.

MAUREEN Enterprise was hoping when they came in here that they would have no bother in Rossport. They were told by their few local supporters that they'd have the opposition sorted out in a few weeks.

VINCENT They saw the people of the area as being compliant. Some years before, an aviation station was built on Dooncarton Hill and there was little or no opposition. So I'm sure Enterprise Energy Ireland was told that there'd be no problem with the gas, that in this place you can do anything because the people are very docile. I suppose from their perspective there was no reason they should have thought any differently. But many people here felt that there had no redress in this case but their own strength and their own moral and physical courage.

WHAT MADE PEOPLE RESIST THE PROJECT?

MAUREEN What set me off first was an experience I had visiting a neighbour. I came upon a woman from the company parked in a jeep in the centre of a narrow road. There was lots of room to move in to the side. But she would not move that jeep until she was ready. I had to sit behind her. I was fuming. I said that if this is what it's going to be like then I don't want it. That really got to me. It was a turning point. In Aghoose I found out that they were going in to fields there, not telling anyone, digging holes and doing what they liked. These were little things but I worried what would it be like when they got to the big things. For example, if you passed their trucks in the morning you'd have to go right in to the side. They wouldn't move. As much as to say 'we come first'.

VINCENT We had a sense that we were under siege and that we were being taken over. We had this feeling that if they got a foothold they would make life so intolerable for us that we'd have to move out. It seemed like they were operating as they would in a Third World country and that they didn't have to ask permission for anything. They acted as if they were the law, as if to show that they were the bosses now.

They would go about in Land Rovers and jeeps and insist on keeping to the middle of the road. I always made them pull in for me. They wore dark glasses and earmuffs and helmets and yellow jackets as part of the psychological campaign they were waging. They took photographs and were always wired and were carrying out surveillance on the local people. For example after they got the injunction in April 2005 preventing anyone from interfering with them they upped the tempo psychologically and would travel along the road, over and back past our house, at about five or ten miles an hour with their hazard lights flashing. In other words, they were saying, 'we got what we wanted and now we can do what we like.' I have no doubt but that these actions were deliberately designed to intimidate us because they were doing no work at the time. I have no doubt about that. It was as if they had got instructions to behave like this. I believe that's what they were trying to do.

A few years before that when the planning application was refused by An Bord Pleanála the reactions from most of the politicians was that this was a terrible day. Black Day for Mayo was the screaming headline in the Connaught Telegraph. The politicians and backers of the project said that a new application must be put in straightaway. It was the same kind of mentality as with the Nice Treaty vote. If we don't get it right the

first time we'll have to try again. So they said the only problem
with the project was how to store the peat deposits. But it was
more than that. The independent inspector of An Bord Pleanála,
Kevin Moore, said it was the wrong project in the wrong place.
The politicians went to work on An Bord Pleanála after that.
They didn't have to worry about Mayo County Council because
they do what they're told. There were short-term appointments
made. We know from the Centre of Public Enquiry Report – The
Great Corrib Gas Controversy – that Shell, Statoil and the Irish
Offshore Operators Association met Bertie Ahern in the
Taoiseach's office on the 15th of September 2003. That was the
night of the big landslide here on Dooncarton Hill. Martin
Cullen and Dermot Aherne were there with An Taoiseach and
then four days later the oil companies and the Irish Offshore
Operators Association had a private meeting with the Chairman
and other members of An Bord Pleanála. I doubt if I'd get a
meeting with the County Manager, never mind with An Bord
Pleanála. And about a week later, Enda Kenny went on local
radio pitching for Shell to reapply. I didn't know at the time
about the Shell and Statoil's meetings but looking at it now the
choreography is obvious. They're all in it together. Kenny's
intervention angered many people and I know that many Fine
Gael supporters were furious. This was at a time when the area
around here was devastated after the Dooncarton landslide.
That's when I wrote to Enda Kenny accusing him of behaving
more like a spokesman for Shell than a representative of his
constituents. The Bishop and the parish priest were taken out
by helicopter to bless the platform I think in 2001. So you can
see that all the major forces were lined up against us – the
Church, the government parties, Fine Gael and big business.

We weren't surprised. But we weren't overawed. We had right
on our side.

MAUREEN At the end of the day who did they think they
were? They were depending on us anyway, on our taxes. You
don't give up. You just have to fight it. Even if you lose you have
just to fight it.

VINCENT What gave us the idea of taking them on and that we
had a chance of winning? I think for me it was that the project
was so wrong. I was appalled that the State which we all believed

is there to protect us was actively siding with Shell against its own citizens and even putting us in danger. That the State was prepared to give away our natural resources was only adding insult to injury. As a community we were being sacrificed just because we were isolated and considered a soft touch. They thought we had no power, that they could just impose this on us. They were going to superimpose a massive industrial complex of over thirty-five acres on a pristine environment. It was clearly the wrong project in the wrong place, as Kevin Moore, the Inspector of An Bord Pleanála, had said. It was going to destroy our area. I was more conscious of that because I had been away. If you looked at the project ahead into the future you could see that it would mean the end of the community and the destruction of a beautiful part of the country. That's what has happened in other parts of the world so why would it be any different here? People would have to move out. Here in Rossport people would have had to leave because Shell would have made life intolerable. It was so wrong that in the next generation and in generations to come, our children and our grandchildren would say, 'This is awful. Look at that monstrosity over there, what did you do about it at the time?' We had to act, especially when we knew that it was wrong. It would be different if you didn't know. You'd have some justification. But when you did know you couldn't live with yourself if you did nothing.

MAUREEN If you think back on all we had when we were young. All the freedom we had. I could play anywhere within this whole area on either side of the estuary. That included the Ballinaboy site. We used play in there half the time. And I thought it was grand. It was like fairyland. It will never be again if this project got in. Think of this area gone forever.

VINCENT Forever! They said that the lifetime of the gas well was about 15-20 years and there's even a section in the EIS about decommissioning the pipeline. They must think we're really stupid to believe that they were going to spend a few hundred million euro on a project that would last for about twenty years. You'd expect a garden shed to last longer than that. We know that there is lots of oil and gas out there in the Atlantic and this is only the beginning. They want a foothold and once they get in they will expand. They already have about 165 Ha

(c. 400 acres) at the Ballinaboy site. This is State forest, which means that it is our forest and Coillte is supposed to be looking after it for us but they did a secret deal with Enterprise Energy Ireland and never consulted with the people. That's just another example of the way we were ignored. Our opposition wasn't just based on personal safety and concerns. The survival of the whole community was at stake.

MAUREEN You realised straight away that you would have to go because it would be far too dangerous to stay.

VINCENT For myself personally I could live with the risk for the rest of my life. There was a good chance that nothing would happen in my lifetime. But I was thinking of the wider community. You could see that gradually they would encroach more and more. I believed that as time went on they would make life so intolerable for us that we would have to move out. When they got the injunction to stop anybody interfering with any of their works it was so broad it could be extended to include almost anything. If I didn't pull in on the side of the road when one of their vehicles approached it could be said I was interfering with their work. The injunction reminds me of a programme I saw about Robert Maxwell, the owner of the Daily Mirror and the man who embezzled pension funds in the UK. He used to threaten newspapers and journalists with an injunction whenever they attempted to write any investigative articles about his activities. I could see Shell using injunctions in the same way. You would really become a slave in your own area. I wasn't prepared to be a slave in my own country. I suppose that's basically why as an Irishman, as an Irish citizen, I was not prepared to derogate sovereignty, or to hand it over, to a foreign company or even to a local company. My safety is not within the gift of the Taoiseach or a High Court Judge for that matter. It's inherent. Its something I have as a person. It is mine. It is my safety. I don't ask anyone for permission to be safe. It is a right. I give my allegiance to the Constitution, not to a politician, or a State company, or an oil company.

They were saying that the pipe was safe despite all the evidence. Minister Dempsey told me in a letter that in the worst-case scenario of the pipeline rupturing and igniting that I would be perfectly safe in my home 70 metres away. That was wrong of course. It was going against all the evidence. If they were prepared to say that then you couldn't trust them. You had to trust yourself. You could see the scenario. The pipe would be installed and their reports would say that it was safe, that the risk of an explosion was infinitesimal. (That's the word Minister Dempsey used). Then in a few years time they would commission another report, a real report this time where they would take the consequences of an explosion into account. This is something they have refused to do in any of their reports so far, even in the Advantica Report. Of course an independent report would find what the Centre of Public Inquiry Report found, that we wouldn't be safe within 400-500 metres of the pipeline in the event of an explosion. They would offer to compensate us or to relocate us. If we didn't accept or move then we would be living here at own risk. There would be a building-free zone here where nobody would be allowed to build or extend within so many metres of the pipeline. So by a process of natural wastage you could then see that fewer and fewer people would be living in the area. In years to come Shell would have the whole area to themselves. I believe that was the long-term plan.

I saw a little boat one day in the Shell compound in Rossport. This may seem very insignificant but it stirred something within me. Maybe it's a throwback to the days of the landlords but I could see situations where they could use an injunction to keep the local people from interfering with them. So you'd have the new landlords fishing the prime spots while the natives would have to keep their heads down. Maybe I'm going a bit too far but if you give some people an inch they'll take a mile.

MAUREEN The compulsory acquisitions meant that we were handing over our land to a private company. That did concern me because it meant that if they can do it here they can do it anywhere. You would not be safe anywhere in the country.

VINCENT They tried to do it here in Rossport. We already saw that the County Council only had a rubber-stamping role as did An Bord Pleanála or Bord Stampála as I call them. We had no confidence in any of the State bodies. We would not get fair play, we would not get justice there. The planning process operates in such a way that the State would get its way. The State is acting for other interests rather than in the interests of the citizen. There is no doubt at all we were betrayed by the main political parties. The Local Authority betrayed us. Those people we elect and pay to look after our interests betrayed us. We were betrayed in the sense that they didn't look at the project properly and they didn't pay any attention to our concerns.

There was a term 'parity of esteem', often used during the peace talks in Northern Ireland but we felt there was no such equality for us when we were dealing with the authorities. The institutions of the State appeared to be leaning over backwards to accommodate Shell. They were facilitators rather than objective neutrals. We felt that our submissions to Mayo County Council and to An Bord Pleanála didn't get due consideration. The County Council didn't surprise us. We believed that the project was too big for them and that they didn't have the expertise. They never had to deal with anything like this before. That still shouldn't have prevented them from getting independent advice. We did have faith in An Bord Pleanála during the first appeal but the second one was ridiculous. In cases of appeals to An Bord Pleanála the planning applications are supposed to be looked anew and in their entirety - de novo. Yet they didn't do that with the second application. They said that we got an oral hearing the last time so there was no need for another. I believe it was a political decision in the end.

Even in the Court the wishes and concerns of Shell seemed to carry more weight than ours. Shell's sworn affidavits were accepted without question even though we would contend that they were lying but we never got a chance to challenge them.

MAUREEN At the beginning it was small things about the project that would hit you. My own life was busy and I had enough to do without this until I got angry on the road. Then, it started to take up my whole time.

VINCENT I don't think though there was that much anger here. That was very important. I think it was controlled. In fact we were very conscious that Shell would love to provoke us. This wasn't going to be won, we weren't going to make any head-way, if we didn't pursue our campaign peacefully and through sound arguments. All we had to go on was our moral authority, our moral courage. We couldn't take them on physically. It was what they wanted. They could then portray us as thugs and as an unruly mob and so on. Then they would have footage that they would use as a propaganda weapon. They reported every 'incident' to the guards. That must be how they operate all over the world. But we kept our discipline and there wasn't one caution or one summons or one arrest or one case where the guards felt they could prosecute. That puts an end to their claims of intimidation.

As evidence of the peaceful nature of the campaign take the Shell compound in Rossport. Even when they put people in jail there was not even a piece of string cut there never mind a piece of wire or damage to property. Here you had only one or two security personnel and there they were in the middle of the night out in the middle of the countryside and yet there was no interference with them. That shows the control that people had and the peaceful nature of the people around here. There hasn't been one incident of a physical nature or damage to property. That's a marvellous record to go by. When the jailing happened people conducted themselves with restraint even though there was a lot of emotion at the time. We were very proud of the people when we were inside. We knew Shell wanted to provoke us.

I think we realised early on that people would go to jail. I suppose if one were to look at it from Shell's point of view once they got the injunction they would have to see it through. They would have to test us out to see if we'd back down. It was common sense. They would have to test out the opposition. They would have to test our resolve, call our bluff. They couldn't have this big project being delayed because of a few people, as they saw it. They'd have to go the whole way. That's what they did.

I'd say before the jailing that many people in the area were indifferent. A lot of people accepted the assurances given by Shell and the politicians about safety and about the milk and honey that would flow once the project was up and running. Many people thought that this small group in Rossport was just causing a bit of a rumpus in order to get more money and that once the compensation was agreed the show would get on the road.

There was a core group of us who were opposed from the beginning on very good grounds because we had done the research and we were not being fooled. We weren't the usual suspects. We hadn't campaigned against any project in the past. They couldn't label us in that way. We weren't NIMBYs either. We knew the project as planned was wrong and dangerous and we didn't want it anywhere else either. Our opponents tried to make out that we were against development. I don't know of anyone around here, or any other place in Ireland for that matter, who is against development. It depends on what you mean by "development". There are many ways in which an area like this can be developed without having a dangerous high-pressure production gas pipelines running several kilometres inland to a massive refinery belching out poisonous emissions through 50-metre-high flaring stacks. There are opportunities here for bird-watching and whale and dolphin-watching. Walking tours are already well developed here and are proving very attractive to tourists. We already have cultural tourism like painting courses and Irish language courses in the Coláistí Samhraidh. People just like to come here and drive around to see the unspoiled countryside. The golf course in Carne has a spectacular view overlooking the Atlantic. How on earth will the present Corrib development plan help to promote these activities?

There were other people besides us who were opposed to what was happening but many felt that they could do nothing about it. They'd love to have been able to do something but somehow they felt powerless. This is very disturbing, that the people who elect the politicians should feel that they have so little say or control over their own lives. I hope that is changing. We should keep reminding ourselves and them that it is we, the people, who have the power and that it is we who are in charge and that we elect our representatives to do just that – to represent us.

MAUREEN That atmosphere is throughout the whole country. You can't do this. You can't do that. And then when they said you can't smoke! Someone said to me when that came in, 'Maureen, this is the end of democracy.' The next few weeks after that they were talking about a tax on fatty foods.

VINCENT Instead of handing over personal responsibility to people for their lives Big Brother appears to be telling us what to do. People feel that somehow they're not as free as they used to be and that they are constantly being dictated to. I have felt for a number of years that this is the general feeling around the country. (I don't wish to sound like De Valera looking into his heart). This was borne out to me from the correspondence we got in jail. A fellow from Donegal wrote to us and said that when he heard we went to jail he was glad. 'Don't get me wrong,' he said, 'but somebody had to do it.' I had that feeling myself for some time before this happened that somebody would have to make a stand. Somebody had to do it. I never thought it would be us. But here was a case where we were justified in standing up. We were fortunate that the issue of safety resonated with people around the country. Yet we were relatively powerless. We weren't a lobby group. We didn't have any resources. All we had was our conviction and our determination.

I felt all along that despite all the hype about the Celtic Tiger and the promotion of greed and individualism in this country that the true nature of the Irish people had not changed. I believe the people are sound, reasonable and compassionate with a sense of fair play, or what we call in Irish Cothrom na Féinne. If I didn't believe in the people then there would have been no point in going to jail because it was the people who got us out. Going to jail was an act of faith in the Irish people and I was proven right because once the people had the facts about what was going on they supported us. Up until the jailing the information and the facts about what was happening were confined to this area. I was hoping that once the facts got out that the people would go along with our analysis.

In early 2005 I wrote to all five Mayo TDs, or public representatives, in Leinster House. I didn't know or hadn't met any of them at that time. I put the facts to them as honestly as I understood them, about how this pipeline and project was different from any other gas project in the rest of the country. The reason I did that was so that they could never say sometime in the future that they didn't know. If it went ahead and proved to be a disaster with dire consequences, they wouldn't be able to wring their hands and say that they didn't know. Jerry Cowley, Independent, came out straight away in support and began to raise the matter in the local media. John Carty, Fianna Fáil, came back to me with a typical answer from the Minister, full of the usual assurances, which I knew to be meaningless. Michael Ring, Fine Gael, also went to the Minister and got the same kind of answer. Beverly Flynn, Fianna Fáil, (now Independent) and Enda Kenny, Leader of Fine Gael, the main Opposition Party, took my letter of concern to Andy Pyle, Managing Director of Shell Ireland. Of course Pyle assured them that everything was okay and that we really had nothing to worry about and that there was a lot of misinformation being put out. He told them that we could all trust Shell. He would, wouldn't he? I found this very disturbing, not Shell's response, but the fact that elected representatives would seek and accept assurances from the head of a private company about the safety of their constituents and moreover that they didn't appear to see anything wrong in asking him in the first place.

Jerry Cowley continued to ask questions and to raise the matter. He came on board when it wasn't a popular thing to do, at a time when there were more votes to be lost than to be gained. This has to be said. As he began to learn more about the project himself he became convinced of the merits of our case. I think that he was impressed by the depth and scope of the research we had done and of the technical knowledge that 'our' side had accumulated over the previous four or five years.

Arising from my letter there was a front-page headline in the Western People – Shell Ignores Safety, Say Residents. Christy Loftus was the journalist and he gave fair coverage to the points I had made. I feel that this article gave the campaign a fresh impetus at a crucial time. Valerie Cox, a reporter for RTE Radio saw this headline during a review of the local papers and she phoned me up. She came down and talked to people. I think it was the first time that the national media took an interest in what was happening to us. I think her report was broadcast on the Today with Pat Kenny programme on the same day as Shell was trying to enter the lands in Rossport.

Things went quiet for a while after that. I knew we'd have to do something. We'd have to go to jail if necessary to bring the issue out into the open, to bring it to the attention of the outside world. And our jailing did have that effect. What was amazing about that was that within a week or two of us going to jail the local people for the first time began to look at the issues and to understand them.

Before, it didn't matter. Many were indifferent. But many came to me after we came out and said, 'We didn't know.' People didn't know what kind of project it was. People were taking

Shell's word and the words of politicians that it was normal. Maybe that is a fault in the Irish people that we are inclined to believe strangers rather than our neighbours and people we have known and worked with all our lives.

What was great about our campaign was that we didn't have a structured organisation. Everyone was welcome and everyone was equal. We had no prima donnas. There was no place for prima donnas in our campaign. From time to time we did have what you might call a primus inter pares. Everybody was prepared to go on and give interviews or talk to the media. Those are people who, including myself, had no interest in seeking publicity and would shy away from a camera or microphone. But now we had to go out and do our bit to tell people that we feared for our safety. Maybe it's because the project was so wrong we were able to overcome our own natural shyness.

Once the commitment was given there was no way you would give up. I couldn't pinpoint the particular moment that I lost fear. It was gradual. I remember saying to a reporter of the Mayo News when we were out on the road during the stand-off last year that when you lose fear you can do anything. That included the prospect of prison or even something more severe, if it existed. There was no fear. It was a gradual process. I wouldn't say there was any one moment. The same process would have occurred for the family and the community as well. We all moved together. I think you lose fear when you have no doubt about the righteousness of your cause, when you know there is so much at stake and because you understand what is at stake that you have a duty to persevere. Whatever it is there is something that makes you rise above it all.

But the toll on many people was terrible. I could see what happened to the people who were living close to the proposed terminal or refinery. After the second Bord Pleanála decision many people felt that that was it, what could they do, it was all over. They must be tired after all those years of fighting against the odds. Would we have thrown in the towel if we lived near the terminal? I'm glad I wasn't there and faced with making that decision. But what happened was that different people came out at different stages of the campaign and by slowing down the project the flaws were exposed. The people of Ballinaboy played their part and it was the cumulative effect of all the efforts that brought it to a standstill.

MAUREEN Furthermore, it was breaking up their families. It has broken up families.

VINCENT Even in our case, the girls would often ask us to talk about something else. Our lives were taken over by the gas. We could hardly talk about anything else. But you could only go to jail with the support of the families. So when the judge expected us to reflect over the lunch hour there was no need for us to reflect. It was obvious what we were going to do. We didn't even have to ask the families - it was understood. Among the family there were no doubts. We were all in it together.

MAUREEN Many of the people here were not used to challenging authority. First, there were the teachers in school. For the older generation you didn't question such people. A lot of people here also were unemployed and depending on a social welfare officer. There was a fear of authority.

VINCENT But there was a loss of fear among those who took a stand here. Many of those who had signed consents did so because they felt there was nothing they could do. They were told that the oil company could take the land anyway. But some landowners didn't accept this and they wouldn't sign and then those of us who were not landowners and who were opposed to what was happening felt duty bound to support those people. So we stood in the field with them when Shell tried to get in. There was no threat of violence even though Shell swore affidavits that they were threatened with violence when attempting to mark out the pipeline route. We never threatened violence. That's what they wanted. We just stood there in front of them. A Garda Sergeant asked me if I was aware that I was breaking the injunction. I said I was. Then he took my name. That was it. If that amounts to violence or the threat of violence then I'm guilty.

MAUREEN We were served then with the injunction. In Brendan's case it was dropped into the boot of his car. He could say he was never served validly.

VINCENT But we didn't use any tactics like trying to find legal loopholes or trying to get off on a technicality. We didn't engage in any sidetracking or delaying tactics. We faced it head-on. For example, it was suggested that we should demand that the case be heard in Irish. But this wasn't about the Irish language. I believe it would have been an abuse of the language to have gone down that road. It was about our safety and the compulsory acquisition of people's land. As I said we faced it head-on.

Enterprise Energy Ireland and later Shell were badly misled by those who thought that they spoke for the people. They were told to go ahead and that there would be very little opposition. At least nothing that couldn't be handled. This campaign has really decapitated those people who once had power in the community. In one fell swoop they've been levelled and now they've gone to ground. Some of the original advocates of the project have now changed their minds but they are not as public in airing their concerns as they were in voicing their support for the project.

MAUREEN The Council for the West was piping up throughout in favour of it. But nobody has elected them. They were never asked to do anything by anyone. Who appointed them? Even those that we do elect like the county councillors have no control over planning. What's the point of having them? The Council is run by an appointed person.

WHAT WAS IT LIKE IN THE LEAD-UP TO THE IMPRISONMENT?

VINCENT The first two occasions that Shell tried to enter we hadn't crossed the Rubicon yet because there was no injunction at that time. They would turn up and somebody would spot them. I remember the first time. This was in January 2005. It was a stormy day. By that I mean a storm-force wind. It wasn't very safe to be out that day. I was in the house and saw someone in a yellow jacket chasing a helmet that was being blown across the road into the drain in front of the house. Then I saw a squad car close behind and a lot of people in close pursuit. It was obvious that Shell personnel were trying to go on to the land. We knew that they would try and we were half expecting them but I didn't think they would come out on such an atrocious day. And they keep telling us that health and safety is their main concern. I didn't know at the time that they had been trying to get on to the farms all morning to mark out the pipeline route. I went down to the road and joined the others. Shell's engineers at this time had gone next door as far as the Mullers' farm and tried to enter but Monica Muller and Peter Sweetman prevented them. We were outside on the road lending support. They failed to put down any marker that day but we knew they'd be back. This meant that we were on edge and constantly on our guard.

The next time they came there was a big media presence with TG4 and Mid-West Radio. Again it was an awful bad day. I went over to Willie Corduff's house that morning. I think we did some interviews. The Shell engineers had already gone on Muller's land with their pegs and cameras and helmets and dark glasses and yellow jackets. They had surrounded Monica and Peter Sweetman who were on their own. They would surround you and try to intimidate you. I noticed on several occasions the way they operated. All their moves seemed to be well rehearsed. There was a group of us on the road looking in. I said to the others that we should all go on to the farm and support Monica and Sweetman. It's amazing how the balance swung in our favour with the extra numbers. They left after a while.

MAUREEN You couldn't see their faces. It would be hard to recognise them.

VINCENT The dark glasses and the whole paraphernalia seemed to be the equivalent of the war paint. The aim was to intimidate. They then went on to Gerard McGrath's land. He's a cousin of Willie Corduff and he lives in England but he hasn't given his consent to Shell to enter his land. Again they tried to put down markers but Willie pulled them up every time. To an onlooker it must have looked like they were shooting a movie scene but this was very real. Then they tried to get into Philip's land. The guards weren't there at that time but somebody called them. In the meantime you had the Shell engineers and us in a stand-off and engaged in a sort of sparring match and local radio and TG 4 were recording the whole conversation. We were talking about the pipeline design code that they were using. I was questioning them about the fact that they were using a code – that's BS 8010 - that was no longer in operation. They asked me was I an engineer. I remarked that Shell would have intelligent pigs (PIG = Pipeline Integrated Gauge) going through the pipeline and that we, the residents, would be the guinea pigs living alongside the pipeline. One of their engineers burst out laughing. He came over to me later and asked me was I Vincent McGrath who plays the accordion. He was an accordion player himself from near Aberdeen and not too far from where the great fiddle player and composer Scot Skinner was born. We had a short chat about music but unfortunately we both had to go back to our respective sides of the divide and wait for the Gardaí to arrive. I said to him, "We won't mention the war". That was the human side. That man is gone from the area now. Refined people like him don't like situations where there is confrontation and they don't stay around for long.

The radio and TV crews were recording everything as it happened. It was very emotive being out on the field. It was like reliving an eviction scene from our history. It must have struck the same chord with the people because when Mid-West Radio replayed the scene over the air the station was inundated with calls supporting us. The voices of the invaders trying to force their way on to the land and the voices of the landowners telling them to get off must have been the most effective history lesson they ever got.

Shell and Roadbridge were not allowed to put down any markers that day either. The next move would have to come from them. They had failed and they would have to get an injunction if they wanted to try again.

Then Shell got their injunction. I think it was in April 2005. So really this would be the test for us the next time they came armed with the injunction. We knew that breaking the injunction would most likely result in jail.

MAUREEN Yet it took the judge a long time to grant that injunction. It took over four days. And at the end he said he didn't know if he was right or wrong.

VINCENT Part of their argument was that they needed the injunction because they needed to start work immediately and every day they were not working was costing them an enormous amount of money. Yet when they got the injunction it took them at least seven weeks before their next attempt to get on to the farms. We didn't know exactly when they'd be back.

The next time they came I was in Belmullet and I got a phone call that they were trying to come in on Brid Mc Garry's land. It was evening time and when I got there there was a large crowd in support. Brid and her mother would not allow them on to their land. Brid's land is across the estuary from where the 3 km of pipes were illegally welded together by Shell. I think everyone in the country has seen that photograph in the papers. They left without getting on to Brid's farm but we were expecting them to arrive in Rossport the following morning.

They came at ten or eleven o'clock in the morning accompanied by the Gardaí. They went on to Philip's land to put down pegs and mark the pipeline route. Philip and his wife Maureen were there on their own and they were surrounded and being bullied and harassed by Shell personnel. There was nobody else around except my daughter, Máire. She went down to the field to support them when she saw what was happening. The Gardaí remained in the car. She asked the guards to come down to the field and protect the people. However, they said they were there to enforce the injunction.

Early next morning they came to Willie Corduff's farm. Mary phoned me and I went over in support. Willie and I stood in front of them as they tried to go on to the land. Shell beckoned to the guards to come and take our names. For me, as an Irishman, it was a pathetic sight to see such fawning servility on the part of the sergeant who took our names. The Shell engineer snapped his fingers and the sergeant almost tripped in his eagerness to get there. I know he had a job to do but he could have shown a lot more dignity. That's how I saw it and it only reinforced my view that Shell wielded great influence in this country and that they would have to be stopped before they got any more control over people's lives.

They had taken a lot of the names – Bríd Mc Garry and her mother, Theresa, Willie Corduff, Mairéad and Liam, Brendan Philbin and his daughter Siobhán, Micheál Ó Seighin, as well as my own name and that of my daughter, Máire. I have great admiration for the young people in particular who showed tremendous courage that day.

Around this time (May–June 2005) Roadbridge (the main contractors) were taking in materials along the narrow road leading to the compound in Rossport. They had taken in portakabins and other materials usually early in the mornings because their big trucks took up the whole road. The Traffic

Management Plan agreed between Shell and Mayo County Council allowed for the roads around the terminal site and the peat deposition site to be upgraded. They had to do this because of the heavy traffic on those roads. But the plan made no provision for the Rossport road and traffic coming into and out of the compound. They estimated that 67 HGVs per day would be using this narrow road over a three-month period. The 'plan' did not involve any consultation with the local people and there was to be no upgrading or widening of the road to allow for any emergency traffic. They were going to do it on the cheap. A large truck and a car could not pass at the same time so the 'plan' was that the locals would have to obey a flagman and wait until the trucks were clear of the road.

One evening two Scania trucks were coming in the Rossport road carrying pipes. Maireád Corduff was on her way out the road and couldn't pass. She stopped and wouldn't reverse. The word went out and about ten cars came and parked up behind her so the two trucks couldn't come in. There was a stand-off for a couple of hours. The guards came then. They asked us to reverse but we refused. They took the names of the car owners and the registration numbers. There was a compromise reached in the end. We allowed the trucks to go in to the compound and turn around without unloading the pipes and we reversed or turned the cars to let them through. They went in and turned around and there was a big cheer. It was seen as a victory for us.

But then they tried it another day after that. Most of our people were in Dublin at the Court. There was hardly anyone around. Máire and Deirdre were coming from Belmullet, (it was about five o'clock) when they spotted a truck loaded with pipes coming in towards Rossport. Suddenly, there was a lot of activity on the road. Flagmen were out and there was a sense that something was about to happen. The girls 'flew' up to the house and told me that the wagonload of pipes was coming towards the compound in Rossport. So we jumped into the car and sped out to the road. I deliberately parked the car along the grass margin and waited for them to arrive. I didn't go in on the grass. There was still place on the narrow road for normal traffic to pass. So I parked there and waited. We could see the truck coming but at this time it hadn't taken the turn on to the road where I was parked. A Shell Land Rover came in the road ahead of the truck and the driver asked me to move the car. The truck still hadn't turned in the road at this stage. I said that I would not move and that I was parking there to highlight the fact there was no traffic management plan for Rossport and that we would be trapped in the event of an emergency. He was in communication with the other jeeps and Land Rovers accompanying the truck. I noticed that the truck had made the turn at this time. So they had made the decision to psych me out and call my bluff. I said to myself, 'This is it. This is confrontation.' I was asked again to move. I said, 'No, I'm parking here.' I pointed out that normal traffic could pass without difficulty and that I was not blocking the road. The truck, a low-loader, came in and decided that it was too dangerous to try and pass as it might heave over in the soft margin. So it stopped and we stayed in the car and waited.

So they parked the truck in front of me and we all waited. We were there about half an hour before anybody came along. It was a long half an hour. There was nobody around. We were there on our own. Then John Monaghan came along and parked behind me. That was like manna from heaven. It was support. Then a few more came. Several Shell and Roadbridge personnel had arrived by now and the place was a sea of yellow. Two squad cars arrived.

The guards were in contact with the superintendent. They wanted us to move. We asked why the truck couldn't reverse. We wondered what law we were breaking. We pointed out that there wasn't any No Parking sign to be seen and that we were not blocking the road since normal traffic could pass. We drove a tractor up beside my car to show that normal traffic could pass without difficulty. We took a photograph for evidence. However, under some section of some Road Traffic Act the guards had the authority to direct traffic to ensure a free flow. So we asked why they weren't directing the truck to reverse. After all they had directed us to move for the Scania trucks the previous occasion. They took our names again. This time we said we wouldn't move. Would we have to be the ones to move the next time, and the next time after that? If we were going to have sixty-seven truck movements over a two-month period would we be the ones to have to move every time. We were not going to do that, so the stand-off followed. The natives were not going to lie down. We were not going to cede the road to Shell or to Roadbridge.

I did offer Shell's engineer the same compromise as before

and that the truck could go in and turn around without unloading the pipes. He refused saying, 'We're going to bring in our materials', which meant he wasn't interested in any compromise. I said in response 'conversation ended', which meant that we were not prepared to move either.

I did say to the superintendent on the previous occasion, and he agreed with me, that in the absence of a proper traffic plan that incidents like this were bound to happen again.

They got another injunction a few days later, this time ordering us off the road. I think what happened next is very significant and marks another turning point in the campaign in my opinion. The injunction named me, Philip, Willie and others and we were being ordered not to interfere with Shell on the road. Here was an order from the President of the High Court more or less instructing us to get out of the way for Shell. There were about twenty people there on the road including women and children the evening the Garda read out the court order. As he was reading it out the people laughed. They didn't even bother to listen. It was a contemptuous and defiant laugh. Now that was very significant. They were showing contempt for a law that was blatantly being used for Shell's benefit and not for their protection. That's how they saw it. They were asking why was the law not protecting them. They said that to the guards, 'What about our rights?' Parity of esteem again. I would see this as a turning point for many in the community because they had decided that they were not going to lie down and they were not prepared to accept laws that were unjust.

The stand-off became important for another reason. It was the first time the people had gathered in a public place to protest and now we had a focal point or rallying point. That became very significant. Up to now we had met in each other's houses. But here was a public rallying point. It was out in the open. People came from all over, from as far as Killala, not a large crowd I must admit, but the word was getting out that we were serious about protecting ourselves. It built confidence. We weren't on our own. This went on twenty-four hours a day for a couple of weeks. People stayed on the road overnight. Here were people making a public statement, making a stand. We had to stay overnight even just to protect their property, so that nobody did any damage or to prevent any agents provocateurs. It was very tiring at the time. We had Bonfire Night on the 23rd June and we lit our bonfire in the bog beside the lorry. We had arranged with the people of Doolin, County Clare that their fire and ours would be lit simultaneously. The bonfire night, or St. John's Night, was always a great community occasion. And now here it was again with a lot more meaning for us. We had reason to protect our community. We realised in a different way what community meant. People here were beginning to talk among themselves and to analyse what was going on and what would happen if the project went ahead as planned. This went on until we went to jail.

COURT AND JAIL

VINCENT We were to appear in the High Court in Dublin on the 29th June. The day before was a very hot day and a very busy one. Some of the men were convinced that there was a septic tank in the compound used by Shell in Rossport and not a storage tank as Mayo County Council had assured us. A septic tank has an outflow pipe and a percolation area. A large crowd had gathered on Brendan Philbin's land beside the compound. We had intended to go in and find out for ourselves whether there was a septic tank there or not. We were taking video footage and recording everything. This was playing them at their own game. Some of the men and women went in to the compound and started to look for the septic tank. I couldn't go in because I didn't have a safe pass and hard hat but we could all see what was happening. They asked our people to leave but they refused. We insisted that Mayo County Council sent down their engineer, Paddy Mahon, and investigate. They were reluctant but we said we would remain there until he arrived. Shell sent for the Gardaí and two squad cars came. They even went out to the cars and brought in the handcuffs and threatened to arrest them. But the men and women held their ground. They then proceeded to uncover the septic tank. Shell must have got word that we were coming because the outflow pipe had been cut and it had been sealed and cemented. They had placed a pallet of concrete blocks over the percolation area. The men removed the blocks and then one of the Shell workers began to drive a JCB as if to help them uncover the percolation area. I realised that they would park the machine over the percolation area if they got that far. So the machine was not allowed to come over. I know I had to go at that stage but they told me that they uncovered the percolation area and that there had been an illegal septic tank there all along. This was more evidence of collusion between Shell and the Council. We didn't trust them then and we don't trust them now.

I remember that I was wrecked that day because the previous night I had been keeping vigil on the road where the truck was stopped and I didn't have much sleep. I went home and tried to get some sleep but something would always come up. As well as that I hadn't even read the court order at that stage. I didn't have any legal representation arranged so I had to try and prepare something for the next day, just in case. But it was a hectic day and I was up again all that night. I did try to snatch an hour before we left but couldn't.

We were to travel to Dublin on Jimmy Barrett's bus at five o'clock in the morning. I said goodbye to the girls and Maureen drove me out the road to where the truck was stopped. We said our goodbye to the gang there and they wished us luck. Maureen didn't travel to Dublin so it must have been a long day for her and for those who were holding the fort at home as they waited for news from Dublin.

It was a terrible bus journey to Dublin that morning. We left at five in the morning. I tried to sleep on the bus but couldn't. I stayed on the bus in Longford and tried to get even ten minutes sleep while the others stopped for something to eat. I was a total wreck. We had no solicitor. Willie and Philip were expecting their solicitors but they never turned up in Court. Here were ordinary people going to the High Court with no legal representation. A case of being thrown to the wolves.

I think Judge Finnegan tried to intimidate us with threats of financial ruin and he threatened to take our houses and our cars and to 'jail every farmer in Mayo' and he told us we'd be in jail 'for a very long time'. You could say he used the nuclear option first. He obviously had no idea what he was dealing with. It wasn't just five individuals being a bit awkward but he was taking on history. He gave us ten minutes to reflect on the consequences after we had refused to purge our contempt. Maybe he was thinking of what the tribunal judge said to Frank Dunlop when he wasn't co-operating. The judge told him to seriously reflect on his position over the weekend and when Dunlop came back he was a chastened man. I was thinking of the case a few weeks before that when the Ryanair boss Michael O'Leary was in contempt of court and the judge kept adjourning the case rather than send him to jail. That's the parity of esteem, or lack of it, I keep talking about. Judge Finnegan then gave our case over to Justice McMannamen to hear after lunch. Maybe they thought that our wives and families would panic and put pressure on us. But they didn't know them either. There was never a chance of that. I remember we did a lot of interviews outside the court and we were very clear about where we stood. We knew going back in there that we wouldn't purge our contempt. I knew we were heading for jail. I was ready for that.

In court I was looking at the court order and I was trying to make out some points. I had had no sleep for a few days. So whatever I said in court I'm sure was disjointed. The point I tried to make to the Justice McMannamen at the time was that for me it was a safety issue and an issue of sovereignty. Being forced to break the injunction was the only option I had if I wished to protect my family. I wasn't prepared to go along with being exposed to the consequences of an explosion. I said I had rights under the Constitution and they weren't being upheld. I said that it is the primary duty of the State to protect its citizens but that this was not happening in our case. I said that my safety was being left in the hands of Shell and that wasn't good enough for me.

That was basically what I said to the judge. But of course I knew he could only give one decision if we refused to purge our contempt of court. I understood that. Before sentencing us the judge went on with the usual stuff, you know, the law must be obeyed, that if people are allowed to disobey the law of the land then there will be anarchy. He was talking about law but we didn't see any justice. Law and justice isn't always the same thing. I think we can vouch for that.

MAUREEN I knew they would be sent to prison because it would be decided on law. Either they broke the injunction or they did not and they had. I knew Shell wouldn't back down. Their idea was that the men would go in for a few days and then would have enough and come out. Máire knew it would happen. Deirdre was hoping something might change at the end. Máire was very angry when the judgement was made.

VINCENT I had been up in the court a few times during the hearings when they were seeking the injunction. You could see that the judge wasn't interested in the safety arguments. He obviously didn't understand that the pipeline in Rossport was different and it seemed like he didn't want to know either.

When the sentence came though, it was still a bit of a shock. We were allowed time to talk to a few people afterwards. I suppose the emotion of it hits you then, when you know the moment is here. The reality is another thing. You were going into the unknown. Unknown for a few reasons – the conditions, the physical conditions, and the duration, the indefinite sentence, and not knowing what support we would get. Would it all peter out after a while? After all it was the summertime, the 'silly season', so we knew that all sorts of things might come into play and take attention away from the jailing and why we were in jail.

There was a big cheer when we left the court to go across to the Bridewell. Obviously this was our first time in the Bridewell and we didn't know that it was a holding cell. There were concrete slabs or 'beds' there about six or seven inches high. There were three of those 'beds' but no bedclothes of any kind. There was an open toilet in the corner with a three-foot wall around it. There was no place to sit so we sat down on the 'beds' on and off for the five hours or so we were there. I think we nodded off from time to time. We didn't know then if this was going to be our prison and if we'd have to endure these conditions for God knows how long. How were we going to cope?

Eventually they gave us a bread roll sandwich and a cup of tea. Then they took us in this prison van or Garda van – the 'sheep box' I think they called it. We knew we were going to Mountjoy. We were actually caged in a steel box – individually of course. It was in total darkness. We couldn't see anything but we called to each other. You just had to look into space. I had nothing with me other than what I was wearing. I had my mobile phone with me and I got a call from Douglas Dalby who wanted to know if I needed anything. I don't remember much of what happened in Mountjoy. I think they took our possessions like money and mobile phones. Anyway it transpired that we wouldn't be staying there and we were taken to Cloverhill Prison. They moved us out that same night. They must have got some calls.

We were weighed and we had our photographs taken and we

saw the prison doctor. There were two cells available when we went into Cloverhill - two three-man cells. I heard only recently that five sex offenders were released to accommodate us. I don't know how true that is. It was decided that myself and Micheál should share a cell and that the other three men would go in together in the other cell. I think the other three decided that it would be better that Micheal and I bored just each other! The cell was about thirteen feet long by nine feet wide. There were bunk beds on one side and the same layout on the opposite side but instead of a bed underneath there was a table and a shelf. This is where we ate our meals. The beds were about two and a half feet wide so this meant that there was about four feet of space between the beds. I'd say the beds were about six feet long. There was about seven feet of space between the beds and the door. There was a toilet and hand basin beside the door but this was an open toilet with just a wall about three feet high on one side between you and the other prisoners – only Micheál in my case. That's the part I think anyone would have found most difficult in terms of privacy. It was very difficult and you never think of things like that when you think of jail. Even if you were in jail with people that you normally live with, say Maureen and myself, it would still be difficult not having your privacy. It could happen that somebody might well be on the toilet when the officers opened the door to check. But no one passes any remark after a while. You make the best of what you have. Everything seemed to be made of plastic – knives, forks, spoons, cups, saucers and plates. Safety seemed to be the priority at all times. You might ask what is the function of the prison officer? Is it to keep the criminals in there and make sure they don't get out and harm the rest of us? When you're in there you realise it's to protect them from each other and from themselves. You want to feel safe in there.

I wasn't shaken or angry or frightened. You had to be level-headed and keep your cool. This could have gone on for a long haul. You didn't know how long. There were so many imponderables there. We didn't know what might happen. So much was out of our control at this stage. All that was within our control was to stay in jail for as long as it took. That was all we could do. I didn't fix on a time in my head for getting out. I was looking on it long-term. I was taking it as it came.

We'd be very aware if there was a rally. The turnout would be important to us. I remember being nervous about the Sligo rally but it was very good. But what was very reassuring was the number of the people coming in to visit. Jerry Cowley was marvellous, extraordinary. He came in to see us time and time again. We didn't have the detail of what was happening outside but we would try and piece it together. We had scraps of information. We had a few strands. First, we had Cowley's visits. We knew there were meetings twice a week locally and he reported back on these. Then there were visits from our families. We also had the daily telephone calls. The calls lasted for six minutes and were monitored but they helped us to piece together what was happening. Micheál would find out something. I would hear something else and we'd all have a chance to talk about in the yard.

There were visits from our local supporters as well. That was important because they were picketing the refinery site at Ballinaboy and Shell wasn't being allowed to do any work. We asked one local man who was picketing the gate if they would stick it out. He said, 'we will stick it out on the outside if ye'll stick it out on the inside.' That was almost a contract! There was an agreement there which was good. They'll do it if we do it. That was very positive. TDs started to come in then. The first thing we got from a lot of the TDs was a question, 'How do we get you out of here?' What they had in mind was some face-saving formula that would make us look good when we climbed down and purged our contempt. The Taoiseach said something similar in answer to a question from a reporter. He said something to the effect that we could come out now – 'They've made their point.' It's a pity he wasn't asked what point did he think we were trying to make. I wonder does he still know? They didn't realise what was going on. We explained that this wasn't about getting out because that was in our own hands. We had to educate them. We had to educate them about the issues and that we knew what we were talking about. We weren't just a few hotheads letting off a bit of steam by going in to prison. We were there to win. We had to win. It was very important to stress this – to win the campaign is essential for our survival as a community.

Newspapers too were important to us. It became clear early on that our issue was very popular. I think we became a cause célèbre. The tabloids surprised us with the coverage and the

'Rossport 5' title seemed to catch on for some reason. We thought it would fade away. That was our big fear, particularly because the Dáil was on holidays. Indeed, I'm sure our imprisonment was deliberately timed to coincide with that. I suppose their reasoning was that people like us liked the open air and that we wouldn't stick it out during a long hot summer and that we'd crack. I just wonder when they began to realise that we weren't going to crack. They must have realised that sometime. It was only when the Dáil was about to come back that they began to move. They knew it was going to be brought up every day in the Dáil.

The rallies were important for us and so was the level of reporting. They kept the story in the top ten news items all summer even through Hurricane Katrina and the bombings in London. In time we started to get letters and cards. We got our post in the evening around seven o'clock when we came in from the yard. In the letters people were saying the same things like 'stick it out,' 'don't give in,' 'you're doing it for us,' 'it's time somebody stood up' – all those themes I had been talking about earlier on and of course lots of talk about corruption. It was quite clear from all around the country that we had a very high level of support. It was very interesting how the Irish language had become important to a lot of people. The people of the Gaeltacht were very angry at the jailing. But many people from outside the Gaeltachtaí too would try and write to us in Irish and others would apologise that they weren't able to write to us in Irish. Maybe they saw this from a nationalistic point of view and that this was old Ireland standing on her feet. Maybe for them the fact that we came from the Gaeltacht gave the struggle and the jailing an extra meaning. I don't know.

I knew that we couldn't give up. It was an imperative that we kept going. If we gave up what chance had other communities again. They would never raise their heads again about any issue if we ended up purging our contempt. It wouldn't have mattered how long we stayed in jail. That was an inspiration, not pressure. We knew that what we were doing was right, that our cause was a just one. It was a national question at this stage. I felt from the letters that we were asserting people's rights and dignity.

It took time to get used to the prison routine. We were not frightened at all of the other prisoners. We got support from the prisoners straight away. They threatened to stage a sit-down protest but we let it be known that we didn't want any disruption. First of all they couldn't understand how we could stay in jail if all we had to do was purge our contempt. After a few days we could see that the message was getting across to them. They understood that it was about a dangerous pipeline and that we were stopping them from coming on to our land. They said that they wouldn't allow that either. They'd say, 'you're right.' If a new prisoner asked us why we wouldn't apologise to the Judge the others would turn on him and explain, 'Can't you see why they're here?' They admired the fact that we could go out whenever we liked but that we weren't going to give in. That seemed to be important to them. We were totally comfortable with them. I suppose we had the social skills to get on with people easily enough. I felt as well from a personal point of view that it was the first time many of them were ever listened to in their lives. They would tell you more and more about themselves and their background and the mess they had got themselves into. Drugs and women seemed to be the source of their problems in many cases. You could see how they had no way out really when they were released. They'd go back to the same environment and they'd be back in. Even within the three months period that we're talking about we saw the revolving door syndrome. Some of them were very young, maybe twenty, with maybe three or four kids. At visiting hours their babies would be brought in. This was very sad to see and sadder to know that nothing was going to change for them. I often thought of what we could do with all the money from our oil and gas that was given away for nothing.

I remember as we were going out of Mountjoy a prison officer suggested that we were going to a better place in Cloverhill. Yet the prisoners told us they'd prefer to be in Mountjoy because there was boredom in Cloverhill. Many of them had been to several prisons all over the country. They said that the day passed much quicker in Mountjoy because of the classes and workshops and that it was more open and that it had a better atmosphere. I knew what they meant about the boredom because there was very little to do in Cloverhill. I'd say that Cloverhill is physically better because it's a much newer building. I think it was built in 1998 but it's a remand prison and prisoners could be there for a few days or a few months waiting for their case to be heard. So it would be difficult to plan classes when you're not sure of the numbers. Also the running of the library there depended on how well staffed they were. If they were short staffed they wouldn't open the library. So the library hours were so irregular that you could have the same books for a few weeks. Then when they opened up you might be on a visit or at something else and you would miss out. There might be a call in the yard – 'library open'. You wouldn't be prepared. You couldn't go back into your cell for your book. You were allowed to take out two books at a time. I must say that the library was well stocked but you would only see a handful of prisoners there. Anyway most of them couldn't read.

When we walked around the yard the other prisoners would greet us with Up the Rossport Five, Keep It Up. They had a phrase – Staunch It Out accompanied by a clenched fist. The prisoners from the other wing would shout out the window. Even at visiting time the prisoners' families would be waving to us from outside the screen in support. The message was out there. It was about common justice. The prisoners saw that. They were very supportive.

Some days were slow especially if it was a wet day. The morning time was the slowest. Breakfast was at a quarter past eight. You might have ten or fifteen minutes to go and collect your breakfast and take it back to the cell. You'd give your name if you wanted a razor or if you wanted to see the doctor or the Governor. We got tea bags, salt and sugar together in a transparent plastic bag and this could do you for a few days. We also got cereal, orange juice and milk and there was plenty of plain bread. The food was nutritious but monotonous. There was a kettle so we could make our own tea. There was a television in the cell too but we didn't watch it much apart from the News. We'd watch TV in the morning over breakfast. Sometimes it would be on the TV3 News about the campaign and the Rossport 5. We could get CNN as well.

During breakfast the warders would come to the door and leave in the razor we had ordered earlier and our names were then ticked off the list. They'd collect the razors about fifteen minutes later and check to see that the blades were still intact and had not been interfered with. At about ten past nine the prison doors were open and you cleaned out the cell. There was a bin for all the rubbish. We put our waste food into the used

milk cartons rather than dumping it straight into the bins.
There was less smell and things didn't look so messy. It was a
lot tidier. You could go then to the lobby and get the bucket and
mop if you wanted to wash the floor of your cell. You have to be
very hygiene-conscious living in an institution, especially in a
prison. We would wash our hands umpteen times a day. I kept
up the habit a long time after coming out. My family noticed it.

We were given two pairs of shorts and two vests and a prison-
issue jumper, a shirt and trousers. The shirt was cotton. The
prisoners would advise us to strop the razor on the shirt to take
the edges off it and prevent us being cut. We could have worn
our own clothes (as could all prisoners) but we made a point of
wearing the prison issue in solidarity with the other prisoners
and anyway we thought it would be more convenient to wear the
prison clothes.

When I went into my bed the first night the spaces between
the slats were full of cigarette ends. Over the next week I had to
empty the whole lot. They didn't clean our cells before we came
in. The smell of cigarettes was terrible and sickening. I used to
smoke at one time but not anymore. The foam mattress was
only about two inches thick and lying on the spaces between
the slats left my back very sore. Some of the prisoners told me
to pack rolled newspapers down in the spaces. I had it covered
with so many newspapers in the end that I couldn't smell
anything. But you were lying on that all the time and we didn't
know how long we were going to be there. It could be two weeks
or two years. We had that kind of feeling.

You'd go out into the yard at ten o'clock. They locked the cells
then. You could go to see the doctor then if you had an
appointment or you could go to the tuck shop. They sold only
loose tobacco and the prisoners would roll their own cigarettes.
They sold sweets, biscuits, drinks, coffee and some
newspapers. On Wednesdays and Thursdays you could order a
Sunday newspaper. If an article appeared in any of the papers
that we hadn't got somebody from the Chaplain's office might
leave it in under our door. There was also a recreation room or
the 'rec'. All that was there was a pool table and I think a TV
room but it was so noisy you'd want to get out of there. I spent
very little time there altogether. We'd be outside in the yard for
about two hours. If we didn't have a visitor that'd be a long time.
On a very wet day you'd have to stand under a shelter and this

was very boring. It was like hanging around in a garage waiting for your car to be repaired. Sometimes you wouldn't have a seat. Also nobody knew the time because we weren't allowed to wear our watches. You'd have to guess. Sometimes we'd ask the officers. Everybody walked anti-clockwise for some reason around the yard. You'd get tired of that. There was a football pitch laid out with goal posts and the prisoners used to play there. You'd have to watch yourself sometimes or you might get your head knocked off with the force of the ball.

We would sit down and read a paper and pass the time and talk to the other prisoners. We were told first to keep to ourselves and to keep our heads down. That would have been a big mistake. I think they believed we'd be there only for a short time. We made a point of going around with the other prisoners and not being together as a group. You'd chat with different people. That was very important. One fellow came in whose brother operated a Shell station but he was an independent. There was a bit of a boycott on at the time. He said that his brother supported us. 'He's with you,' he said. He thought that a boycott could hurt people who supported us. I agreed with him. There was one prisoner there who couldn't understand how some people could beg for money in the street. 'Why don't they go and rob a car or do something else instead of begging,' he would say. He had this strange logic – that stealing from a car was acceptable but begging was shaming your family. 'I tell them never to do that,' he would say.

It was a very positive experience being with the prisoners. Many of the men there couldn't raise bail of even €200. Yet others were able to raise €30,000 and were released on bail. Laissez-faire or the market forces in operation, even in prison! You'd love to give them €200 but you couldn't do it for everyone. Anyway you cannot save the world. There was no gap or gulf between us. They all identified with us, those from the country and the city. And the prison officers were very courteous and professional. I wouldn't use the word 'screw' when talking to the prisoners about the officers.

The occasional journeys to the court were a big help. It was important to get out. Every time we went out there was media interest. It was good for our supporters as well and we also had a chance to meet our families. It would reinforce them. Reporters would be there and you'd see something in the newspapers afterwards. All that helped to keep up the morale and to keep the campaign alive. We were amazed at how it had taken off, how it had captured the imagination. Amazed but obviously pleasantly surprised as well. Most of the press was very favourable. There was one article in a Sunday newspaper that tried to do a hatchet job on us and on the community in Rossport by trying to portray us as backward, lazy – the usual. The journalist failed to realise that the days of pitching East against West are gone. As Liberace is supposed to have said about someone, 'I'd mention his name but I don't want to make him famous!' The people of Dublin were among our strongest supporters. People in the inner city identified with us very clearly. They were small people who were used to being walked on all their lives and of being misrepresented or not represented at all. We were in the same position. There was no town and country divide. The support we got in Dublin was phenomenal. I think that's what frightened them.

We got our dinner at around twelve o'clock noon. This was very early but we got used to it. We had a small snack at about four o'clock in the afternoon and then evening supper, which consisted of two half pint cartons of milk, at about seven o'clock. You had to be a squirrel and have some food stored for the night. You could put on weight very easily there. You'd have to be very careful. I used to ask for small portions – a very unusual request. I suppose that the food has improved from the time of Oliver Twist. The serving staff would look at you wondering if you were okay. You're not using your muscles really either. You're not climbing or doing anything very physical. You're not going on long walks. You walk around but you're not using very much energy. So the only way you can manage is to cut down on food.

We got our post after supper. We used to have to share our post because the other men next door would want to have some of it. We'd swap the next day. The letters and cards were very supportive and this gave us great encouragement. We were locked up from after seven in the evening until a quarter past eight in the morning – thirteen hours. We didn't bother with any films or late night programmes on TV because that would upset our routine. Routine was very important. Saturday and Sunday you could have a lie-in in that you didn't have to get up for breakfast. But in our cell we treated Saturday and Sunday the same as any other day. You'd be on a slippery slope if you broke your routine. You had to be consistent.

I'm sure that we were being monitored and that our actions and our behaviour were being reported back. Back to where exactly I don't know but back to someone up the ladder. I'm convinced that they were monitoring us – our resolve and all that. I have no doubt it was being reported back by officers and probably by prisoners as well. But we didn't have anything to hide. We'd say the same thing in whatever situation we found ourselves. That made it easy from our point of view. We didn't have to pretend about anything.

The family visits were very difficult because we saw each other through a screen. We weren't allowed to touch. A morning visit wasn't too bad. If they could get in for ten o'clock it would be quiet enough, but after that the place could be very noisy with kids. You'd have to shout then through the screen to be heard. I got a "box visit" (which is classed as a private visit although there's a prison officer present) after Deirdre got her Leaving Certificate results. But otherwise I wouldn't ask for box visits.

MAUREEN I was never very good at speeches but during the summer it just had to be done. When you have to do something you do it. If you stopped to think about it you mightn't. The day they went in we thought it was possible that they might be out the next day or the next week. But as time went on we realised that it was going to be long. Regarding the court I was very angry. Deirdre was more upset, but Máire also was angry. They understood very well why this was happening. They wouldn't have been in favour of them purging their contempt and coming out. Nor would any of the children of the other men. The young people were great. The day they went in we didn't know what was happening. I wasn't in Dublin so I was relying on Caitlín and Mary to keep me in touch as to what was going on. I was going to go up the next day but they said to wait until we see where they are. The blockade of the lorry was still going on out on the road. It was our car that was there. So I had to deal with Shell to move the car. That was over the following weekend.

We were very scared of the rallies at the beginning. Particularly the rally in Belmullet because you didn't know how many would turn up. The first rally in Castlebar was very good.

We had been anxious beforehand. Everything hinged on the support we could get. Also there were people coming to the support camp that had been set up locally. They didn't know where to go so they had to be accommodated as well. They set up in front of the house here. The conditions were awful because it was just a bog. There is no praise high enough for them.

Ballinaboy was the best aspect. To see so many locals coming out and picketing the gates! There were old people and everyone lining up. That happened on the Monday after the imprisonment. Everyone there knew that they too could have been imprisoned. There were hundreds there. A lot of those who had favoured the gas came out and supported us. We had thought they would try to get the pipes put down when the men were in prison. We thought that was the whole purpose of putting them in.

The wives had to get on with it and deal with the media. It was hard to keep up with it. In the morning there might be somebody and an hour later somebody else and it was hard to keep track of it. You hadn't time. They might come taking photographs or filming and it could take an hour with you walking back the road until they got the shots right, walking the way they wanted you too. You just did what you had to do.

VINCENT I think the best thing that everyone did was to accommodate the media and to give as much time to a local magazine as to say the BBC. I don't think that anybody was ever refused for interview. We always facilitated them if we could. If you couldn't do it yourself you'd get someone else to do it. We owed it to them because we always complained that we didn't get media coverage early on. So when the media came we did our best to accommodate them. Maureen had to travel all over the place.

MAUREEN There was a lot of travelling up and down to Dublin. You'd have to leave at four or five in the morning. The new road wasn't open then. I didn't really know where I was going in the beginning because I had never had to go up to Dublin on my own. We were lucky that Cloverhill was on this side of Dublin. There were a few times that I went up where I'd be waiting an hour and a half before getting in. That was a long time waiting. You'd leave something in for him and he might never get it.

The worst thing was not knowing when they were coming out. Exam results – all these things were coming along then. Back to school in September or October – that all had to be sorted out along with everything else. I knew they wouldn't come out until the injunction was lifted. Máire was thinking of not going back to college. She wanted to take a year out. But I didn't want her to. I tried to explain to her that she'd be better off in Dublin where it was easier to visit the prison. So she decided to keep on.

VINCENT When we came out it was straight back into the campaign. We were exhausted. It was back to watching the road again. We had no break at all.

HOW WAS IT AT THE RELEASE?

VINCENT Efforts were being made from the start with various mediators being proposed. But it was clear to them that we were not going to purge our contempt. What that would have meant is that we'd have to go back home and look on as Shell went ahead and laid the pipeline. It was quite simple – we couldn't purge our contempt. We couldn't allow them to do that.

We had some inclination of the release the day before. Though it was sudden it was all choreographed in the end. One of the prison officers said something to us the day before that it might happen. We were wary because on a few occasions before we were told that this might be it but it turned out to be a false alarm. There was a bit of confusion in the court the day we were released. It wasn't clear to everyone if we were being let out. There was a guard sitting behind me in the courtroom – there was a guard assigned to each of us – and I turned around and asked him, 'Am I going back with you? Am I free to go?' I didn't know exactly what had happened. He said, 'No, you're free. You can go.' Then I realised it was over. I could see people breaking down with sheer joy. There was such relief. Maureen and Máire and Deirdre were very emotional and why not? They had suffered more than I had because they had to make those long journeys to and from Dublin to visit me. Maureen had travelled all over the country to attend rallies and meetings. But they had remained so strong and so resolute all through. I was very proud of them and I was very proud of all the people who stood by us. There was so much emotion around the day we were released.

MAUREEN When they got out it was crazy. First, they had no clothes. Máire had to go off and buy him a shirt and a pair of jeans. He came out in the same suit as when he went in which probably was filthy by then.

VINCENT I don't think I'll ever wear that suit again. My suit was clean. You could get your clothes cleaned anytime in prison. They were very good like that.

MAUREEN People were great in Dublin – especially the taxi-drivers. Some of them had stickers up on their cars. They were a great source of information for other people.

I got a call the night before that the injunction might be dropped. I was in Galway that evening at a meeting in NUIG. That's all I knew. I wasn't sure really. Then it came on the news while we at the meeting that there might be a breakthrough. Halfway through this talk everybody knew that something was happening. Then after it they were all at me trying to find out. I didn't know any more than they knew. The public probably thought I knew but I didn't. I thought if I said anything people might only be let down in the morning.

VINCENT I think what attracted the public to our campaign throughout was the dignified way our people conducted themselves. I've heard people refer to it again and again. People made so many sacrifices. Everybody that helped in the campaign made a sacrifice. That includes the people who came out to the rallies and to the meetings, people from different parts of Ireland who never met us or knew us. It includes the people who made posters. They were just as important as we were. Politicians take notice of numbers and it was the growing numbers that frightened them in the end.

MAUREEN The men were locked up. There was only so much they could do.

VINCENT It was a collective effort. There's no doubt about that. Different people came along at different times. I came along at a certain point and my forte was research. While others may have dropped out at particular times over the six years they were important at a particular stage of the campaign.

MAUREEN In terms of the campaign there is as much to be done now as there was this time last year. The difference is that you can choose your time more than last year.

VINCENT We're as busy now as we ever were because despite all the spin nothing has changed and Shell and the Government are still trying to force this project on us. I suppose it's not true to say that nothing has changed because support for our stance has grown and our determination has grown. Now there is a different context because people understand the arguments about safety and they know that their oil and gas was given away for nothing and they know that they are not going to benefit in any way.

If they try to put people in jail again I think the people of Ireland will be twice as angry. The people of Ireland already told them last year that they went too far when they put people to jail. They were saying 'This isn't right, you can't do this.' If they're foolish enough to try it again I think the people would say to them, 'We told you before that you shouldn't have put people in jail before, so why are you doing it again?' People can tolerate so much but jailing ordinary people for defending themselves was the last straw.

MAUREEN I was always afraid that it could get violent.

VINCENT We were afraid of agents provocateurs at the rallies. But you didn't have any of those elements at our rallies, any rowdy elements, that would have made that possible. They'd stand out like a sore thumb. The policing was light. The guards and authorities knew that there wouldn't be any trouble from our supporters. But beneath that sunny exterior there was steely determination.

MAUREEN The guards that were sent here to Ballinaboy to supervise the pickets were absolutely delighted. They were getting overtime and there was nothing for them to do here. It was all very peaceful.

VINCENT When we were released though we couldn't believe it. It was raining outside but we hardly noticed. We stayed around outside the court for a few hours just after we came out. It was hectic having to deal with all the media attention. I don't know how many interviews I did that day. I think we gave everyone time for interviews and to take photographs. That night we went on The Late Late Show. There was an incredible level of interest afterwards. There were photographers on the steps outside the RTE studio. Our wives had been on the Late Late Show during the summer and made a great impression. That's the feedback we got. Again, there was no ranting, it was very dignified. It was ordinary people being dragged out of their everyday lives, out of their natural environment, and thrust into the limelight. I think people empathised with them.

MAUREEN Someone wrote a review about the clothes we were wearing, that we were so dolled up. I thought I wasn't half-dressed!

VINCENT The journey home was amazing. It seemed to be a big story on the local radios as we drove across the country. There was live coverage on Mid-West Radio and the event was being broadcast as a triumphant homecoming. They kept playing requests for us. We stopped in Longford for something to eat. Crossing the Shannon seems to have been another symbolic moment and then we saw bonfires at different towns and villages along the way. Radio Mid-West interviewed us live when we arrived in Crossmolina. I remembered to say a few words to the Irish abroad as it was going live out on the Internet. The nearer we got to home the more bonfires we saw and the motorcade lengthened. It must have been about two o'clock in the morning when we got to Ballinaboy. The scene there was amazing. A huge crowd were waiting patiently all night for us to arrive. They were gathered right in front of the refinery gate. The location they chose was interesting. They were making their own statement. I can't put into words what it was like. You could see how the mood had changed and that people now realised that it wasn't just about a few people in Rossport. It concerned them too. There was hugging. There were tears. There was pride. One woman said to me, 'They gave ye back to us.' I thought that phrase was very, very emotive. I felt she was saying, 'You're one of ours. You belong here. What they do to you they do to us.' It was as if we had been taken away, wrenched away from the community, the extended family. There were echoes in that remark of snatch squads in other parts of the world or a folk memory of things that happened in our own history. I think the use of 'they' says it all, that 'they' are not one of us, not one of ours, 'they' are foreign. We were all tired and emotional that night. If someone asked me what was my strongest emotion that night I'd have to say it was pride. I was proud of the people who had gathered there almost in silence. There was no shouting or ranting. These were people who had been neglected and lied to for generations, people who had to emigrate in their thousands, yet you could almost touch their dignity.

The next day we had a rally in Ballinaboy. Again a large crowd gathered and people were much more relaxed. We set off on the road to Dublin that afternoon to attend a concert in the Ambassador.

About a fortnight later there was a concert in Belmullet, which was a fantastic event. Eight or nine hundred people turned up that night. It showed the level of support we had. People had swung around when they understood the issues and they began to realise that so much about the gas project was propaganda and spin. They also saw the danger. And they would say to us 'We didn't know. We didn't understand.' We all said a few words and I remember saying on the night that there was a great feeling of togetherness which reminded me of the meitheal long ago. I felt that the people of Erris were together again as a community.

WHAT ABOUT THE FUTURE?

VINCENT The Shell project here is gone, at least the idea of a production pipeline connected to an onshore refinery. There is no recovery for Shell here. We cannot trust them. There are so many instances around the world – the latest one in Scotland – where they have been lax on safety. Valves have failed. All those things tell us that they cannot be trusted to protect us. They have failed on other projects. They will claim they are bound by certain standards but we don't trust them. We don't trust any of the authorities to monitor them on our behalf. The bottom line is we trust ourselves to protect our environment and to protect ourselves. We are the people who live here. It makes sense that we are the ones who have the interest of our environment at heart. This is where we live and where we want to live and live safely. There is no chance now of Shell coming in here at all.

This whole experience has reinforced my belief that the Irish people have a sense of justice and that they will stand up for what is right and that they will not be pushed against their will. People aren't going to go to jail lightly. People don't just go to jail without good reason. They do so only when they feel strongly and when the law and the authorities have failed them. It's up to the government and the State and the authorities to listen to those people and to take their concerns into account. I think people will assert their dignity and their rights more and more and I think the governments will have no choice but to listen. I think that's the big lesson.

The rural community here has been radicalised, particularly those people who always voted Fianna Fáil or Fine Gael and who are now saying that they will not vote for them again. Another thing is that the women have been politicised. Women may be slow to get involved in social and political campaigns but when they do they won't let their bone go with any dog. And maybe they're slower to compromise as well.

We're keeping the campaign focused on the one issue of safety all the time. As it happens our instinct or our common-sense has guided us along without any political or PR training. When you have right on your side you don't have to spin.

MAUREEN We also had a very wide network of contacts throughout the country from different things – music, work, and so on. If you never left home you wouldn't have had that. In a successful campaign you have to know exactly what you want.

VINCENT Other campaigns might have settled for something less than the main objective. Maybe that was the important thing for us – we couldn't compromise. We couldn't settle for half or three quarter's safety. The lines were very clearly drawn for us in such a way that we couldn't let this happen. It would be the end of a community. Shell picked the wrong place.

There are echoes of things in the past too. There was more solidarity here than people realised. Many people thought there was this individualism that had taken hold in the country and that people wouldn't come and support their neighbour. But the sense of community was always strong here and neighbours always helped each other at busy times of the year like when cutting and saving the turf and at harvest time. This is called the meitheal.

I believe another thing that was very important for us was that we stuck to the main issue of health and safety. It wasn't about money even though our opponents tried very hard to give that impression. I think that people were pleasantly surprised by this. It took a long time though to convince a lot of people that it wasn't about money. I don't blame people for thinking that way because in too many cases they have seen people putting money before principle. I think this has left a lot of people disappointed and disillusioned. Most people around the country were sick and tired of sell-outs. People giving them hope for a short while only for their hopes to be dashed again. That's why people may have withheld judgement on us for a long time, trying to figure out what we were really after.

But in our case neither the Government nor the oil companies could buy our dignity nor could they buy our freedom.